The
K.I.S.S.
Principle

The
K.I.S.S.
Principle

Keep It Simple Servant

A Guide to the Simplicity of Salvation

Rev. Clayton Hampton

XULON ELITE

Xulon Press Elite
2301 Lucien Way #415
Maitland, FL 32751
407.339.4217
www.xulonpress.com

© 2017 by Rev. Clayton Hampton

All rights reserved solely by the author. The author guarantees all contents are original and do not infringe upon the legal rights of any other person or work. No part of this book may be reproduced in any form without the permission of the author. The views expressed in this book are not necessarily those of the publisher.

Unless otherwise indicated, Scripture quotations taken from the King James Version (KJV) – *public domain*.

Printed in the United States of America.

ISBN-13: 978-1-54561-819-6

DEDICATION

This book is dedicated to my lovely wife, Joy, without whom I would probably never have attended a Bible School that focused so much on a clear and concise presentation of the gospel of the Lord Jesus Christ. I am not only grateful, but am deeply indebted to her for putting me in a position to not only be knowledgeable in this area of great concern, but for enabling me to lift the banner of simplicity so that others can present the gospel with as much clarity and simplicity as possible, as God intended, and thus see more souls won to the Lord.

Thank You Sweetie.

I Love You.

TABLE OF CONTENTS

Part I:
Misconceptions of Mankind
(In regard to non-Christian beliefs...) 1
Salvation according to Islam. 2
Salvation according to Hinduism 5
Salvation according to Buddhism. 7
Salvation according to Confucius 8
Salvation according to The Baha'i Faith 10
Salvation according to Scientology. 14
Salvation according to Atheists and Agnostics 17

Part II:
Misconceptions of Religious Variants
(In regard to distorted Christian so-called beliefs...) 21
Salvation according to Jehovah Witnesses 22
Salvation according to Mormons 26
Salvation according to Seventh Day Adventism. 31
Salvation according to Christian Science and Unity. . 32
Salvation according to the Children of God 36
Salvation according to Sun Yung Moon 39
Salvation according to Judaism 41
Salvation according to Unitarians. 45
Salvation according to Masons. 47

Part III:
Misconceptions of Christendom
(In regard to Christian beliefs...) 51
Salvation according to Catholicism. 52
Salvation according to Protestantism. 57
Salvation according to Calvinism 57
Salvation according to Armenianism 65
Salvation according to Lutherans. 68
Salvation according to Episcopalians. 70
Salvation according to Baptists 74
American Baptist Association 74
Northern/American Baptists. 78
Southern Baptists 83

Independent Baptists. 89
Free Will Baptists. 93
Salvation according to Methodists 95
Salvation according to Presbyterians 106
Salvation according to the churches of Christ 111
Salvation according to the United Church of Christ. . 116
Salvation according to the Christian Church 119
Salvation according to Pentecostals. 121
Salvation according to the Church of God 126
Salvation according to The Church of the Nazarene . 131
Salvation according to Christian Organizations 138
The World Council of Churches 138
The National Council of Churches 139
The Fellowship of Christian Athletes 145
Campus Crusade for Christ. 147
InterVarsity Christian Fellowship 150
The Navigators. 155
Teen Challenge 159
Youth for Christ 166
Salvation according to Evangelistic Organizations. . 168
The American Bible Society 168
The American Tract Society 169
Billy Graham Evangelistic Association. 171
Child Evangelism Fellowship. 174
Gideons International. 183
The Gospel Coalition 187
Salvation according to Family Organizations 189
Awana Clubs 189
Focus on the Family 193
Promise Keepers. 196
Salvation according to Missions and Outreach 201
Organizations. 201
Habitat for Humanity 201
New Tribes Mission 202
The Salvation Army 203
Jews for Jesus 206
Operation Mobilization. 210

Part IV:
Concept of Scripture
Keep It Simple Servant
(In regard to God's plan for simplicity...) 213
    Recommended Reading. 221

FOREWORD

The secular world gets the sanctity of life and the sanctity of marriage wrong. The Church often gets the correctness and clarity of the Gospel of Jesus Christ wrong. Clayton Hampton in his new book, **The K.I.S.S.(Keep It Simple Servant) Principle** *doesn't get it wrong. Instead, he lays out the case for the simplicity of the gospel without adding incorrect or unclear information to the gospel nor removing its heart beat...the death and resurrection of Jesus Christ as the satisfactory and sufficient payment for our sins. Then, Clayton carefully and kindly identifies the message of salvation taught by many Christian ministries and various cults and world religions with the intention of revealing their error.*

You will find **The K.I.S.S.(Keep It Simple Servant) Principle** *a "must-read" for those who seriously want to know the Gospel of Jesus Christ for the purpose of communicating the message of*

The K.I.S.S. Principle

salvation by grace alone, through faith alone, in Christ alone, for the glory of God alone in a manner that is correct, clear, courageous, compassionate... and simple!

Dr. Stan Ponz, President

Florida Bible College

Orlando, Florida

INTRODUCTION

One of the most severe misconceptions of the "Religious Community" today that has come down through the ages is the varied emphasis on and understanding of Eternal Salvation and/or Eternal Life and just how to attain it. While all of Christendom focuses on Jesus Christ as the way to salvation, there appears to be a wide range of courses and/or so-called plans containing various steps as just how to attain the aforementioned salvation through Christ. It is with these thoughts in mind that this book has been written, not as a source of antagonism for your current belief, but to lay waist the various difficulties, misconceptions, rules, regulations, and misunderstandings that man has brought to bear on this most important teaching in scripture and simply apply The K.I.S.S. Principle, allowing all to have an easy to understand approach to this great truth...

The K.I.S.S. Principle

Lest you be disillusioned with the scriptural answers provided to the various doctrines and/or beliefs set forth in this communication as being false, simply because they may be diametrically opposed to your current approach to this subject, it may be a good idea, at this point, to remind the reader of God's concern for simplicity and Satan's ability to keep us from it, as was stated by the Apostle Paul in his second letter to the Church at Corinth...

But I fear, lest by any means, as the serpent beguiled Eve through his subtilty,

so your minds should be corrupted from the simplicity that is in Christ.

~ 2 Corinthians 11:3

DISCLAIMER

This book was not written nor intended as a source of antagonism, but as an admonition to simplicity. If you are not spiritually prepared to be objective in your review or approach to the subject matter contained herein as opposed to your current position on the subject, then you probably shouldn't read this book.

PART I

MISCONCEPTIONS OF MANKIND

In regard to non-Christian beliefs…

While the focus of this book is not to delve into the various religious beliefs of mankind in depth, I feel that it is important to elaborate on a small part of this information to provide a clearer understanding of not only the problem at hand, but the reason why it is so important for us to understand the message that has been passed down to us in the simplest terms possible. Keep in mind that one of Satan's goals is to '…corrupt our minds from the simplicity that is in Christ.'

In General, while there are those who say that they do not believe there is a God, the vast majority of mankind not only believes in God or, that is, a

The K.I.S.S. Principle

supreme being, but also believe in an afterlife that includes two primary places, a place of eternal bliss called by most Heaven and a place of eternal torment called Hell. There are probably almost as many varied views of these places and of the so-called God they believe in as there are people or that is peoples of the earth.

Salvation according to Islam

There are those who believe that Muhammad's teachings are the way to Allah as a part of the Muslim faith.

> For a Muslim, the purpose of life is to live in a way that is pleasing to Allah so that one may gain Paradise. It is believed that at puberty, an account of each person's deeds is opened, and this will be used at the Day of Judgment to determine his eternal fate. The Qur'an also suggests a doctrine of divine predestination. [1]

> The Muslim doctrine of salvation is that unbelievers (*kuffar*, literally "those who are ungrateful") and sinners will be condemned, but genuine repentance results in Allah's forgiveness and entrance into Paradise upon death.

---

[1] Qur'an 4:49, 24:21, 57:22.

The Qur'an teaches the necessity of both faith and good works for salvation:

He it is Who sends blessings on you, as do His angels, that He may bring you out from the depths of Darkness into Light: and He is Full of Mercy to the Believers.(33:43)

In the case of those who say, "Our Lord is Allah," and, further, stand straight and steadfast, the angels descend on them (from time to time): "Fear ye not!" (they suggest), "Nor grieve! but receive the Glad Tidings of the Garden (of Bliss), that which ye were promised!"(41:30)

And fear the Fire, which is prepared for those who reject Faith. (3:131)

It is not righteousness that ye turn your faces towards East or West; but it is righteousness to believe in Allah and the Last Day, and the Angels, and the Book, and the Messengers; to spend of your substance, out of love for Him, for your kin, for orphans, for the needy, for the wayfarer, for those who ask, and for the ransom of slaves; to be steadfast in prayer, and give zakat; to fulfill the contracts which ye have made; and to be firm and patient, in pain (or

The K.I.S.S. Principle

suffering) and adversity, and throughout all periods of panic.(2:177)

You be foremost (in seeking) forgiveness from your Lord, and a Garden (of Bliss), the width whereof is as the width of heaven and earth, prepared for those who believe in Allah and His messengers: that is the Grace of Allah, which He bestows on whom He pleases: and Allah is the Lord of Grace abounding."(57:21)

Those are limits set by Allah. those who obey Allah and His Messenger will be admitted to Gardens with rivers flowing beneath, to abide therein (for ever) and that will be the supreme achievement. But those who disobey Allah and His Messenger and transgress His limits will be admitted to a Fire, to abide therein: And they shall have a humiliating punishment.(4:13-14)

To those who believe and do deeds of righteousness hath Allah promised forgiveness and a great reward.(5:9)

But those who believe and work righteousness,- no burden do We place on any soul, but that which it can bear, they will be Companions of the Garden, therein to dwell (forever). (7:42)

Rev. Clayton Hampton

As to those who believe and work righteousness, verily We shall not suffer to perish the reward of any who do a (single) righteous deed.(18:30)

But after them there followed a posterity who missed prayers and followed after lusts soon, then, will they face Destruction,-Except those who repent and believe, and work righteousness: for these will enter the Garden and will not be wronged in the least,-Gardens of Eternity, those which (Allah) Most Gracious has promised to His servants in the Unseen: for His promise must (necessarily) come to pass." S. 19:59-61[2]

Please note that the teachings of this belief involve not only faith, but the consistent works of the individual to attain the place of bliss provided by Allah.

Salvation according to Hinduism

Salvation for a Hindu is called Moksha. Moksha is when an enlightened human being is freed from the cycle of life-and-death (the endless cycle of death and reincarnation) and comes into a state of completeness. He then becomes one with God.

---

[2] Purpose of Life and Salvation in Islam at: http://www.religionfacts.com/islam/beliefs/salvation.htm#1

The K.I.S.S. Principle

There are four ways to Moksha:

1. The Way of Action: This involves carrying out certain religious ceremonies, duties and rites. The objective is to perform works without regard for personal gain.

2. The Way of Knowledge: This requires using your mind and philosophy to come to a complete comprehension of the universe.

3. The Way of Devotion: Salvation is reached through acts of worship, based upon the love for a God (there are thousands of gods in Hinduism).

4. The Royal Road: The use of meditation and yoga techniques. This method of reaching salvation is typically only used by wandering monks.

Each of these ways to salvation in Hinduism requires that a person do certain things. Salvation is through what a Hindu does. It is through human works.[3]

---

[3] Salvation in Hinduism at: http://www.evangelical.us/hinduism.html

Salvation according to Buddhism

There are those who believe that the teachings of Buddha are the way to eternal bliss.

Buddhism developed out of Hinduism in the sixth century B.C. For a Buddhist, salvation is reaching Nirvana. Nirvana is a transcendental, blissful, spiritual state of nothingness. You become a Buddha.

To reach Nirvana you must follow the Noble Eightfold Path. The Nobel Eightfold Path is:

1. Right Understanding: accepting the Four Noble Truths. (The existence of suffering; the cause of suffering; the end of suffering; and the end of pain.)

2. Right Resolve: renounce the pleasures of the body. Change your lifestyle so that you harm no living creatures and have kind thoughts for everyone.

3. Right Speech: do not gossip, lie or slander anyone.

4. Right Action: do not kill, steal or engage in an unlawful sexual act.

5. Right Occupation: avoid working at any job that could harm someone.

The K.I.S.S. Principle

6. Right Effort: heroically work to eliminate evil from your life. Through your own effort develop good conduct and a clean mind.

7. Right Contemplation: make your self aware of your deeds, words and thoughts so that you can be free of desire and sorrow.

8. Right Meditation: train your mind to focus on a single object without wavering so as to develop a calm mind capable of concentration.

Following the Noble Eightfold Path requires that a person do the above eight things. Salvation is through what a Buddhist does. It is through human works.[4]

Salvation according to Confucius

There are those who believe that following the teachings of Confucius is the way to attain not so much eternal bliss, as that of bliss on earth:

> For 2,000 years Confucianism was the official philosophy of China. The only way a person could achieve an important position in the government or in society was by having a good knowledge of Confucianism. To become a

---

[4] Salvation in Buddhism at: http://www.evangelical.us/buddhism.html

government official it was necessary to pass a difficult civil service examination based on the ideas of Confucius. Since it was Confucianism that kept the leaders in power, they were opposed to any changes. The Confucianists believed that they were the only civilized community in the world and they looked down on the beliefs and cultures of other people. This attitude made the Chinese unwilling to change their way of life when they were first exposed to Western culture. This unwillingness to adopt Western ideas and techniques in the late 19th and early 20th centuries proved to be disastrous for the Chinese.

Confucius himself was not very interested in the ideas of a God, an after life, heaven, and other ideas that we associate with religion. However, when Confucianism became the official philosophy of China, religious functions were incorporated into it. Confucius, together with his ancestors and famous followers, became objects of worship. Confucian temples were built all over China and sacrifices and rituals were performed.[5]

---

[5] The Importance of Confucianism at: http://www.globaled.org/chinaproject/confucian/reading1.html

The K.I.S.S. Principle

Salvation according to the Baha'i Faith

However, the beliefs that appear to be most puzzling to me are the ones like the Baha'i faith that believe that while there may be one God, that different people call Him different things and thus have different ways to get to Him, but say that they will all get there. In their case, you may best understand their belief as illustrated by the look of a wagon wheel, where the center of the wheel represents God and the spokes of the wheel represent the different beliefs that grant access to God. Put simply, according to this belief, all beliefs in God, though He is known by different names, lead to the same person and/or place.

> The **Bahá'í Faith** is a monotheistic religion(In theology, **monotheism** (from Greek μόνος "only" and θεός "God") is the belief that only one God exists.[6]) founded by Bahá'u'lláh(**Bahá´u´lláh** (*ba-haa-ol-laa*, Arabic: بهاء الله "Glory of God") (12 November 1817 – 29 May 1892), born **Mírzá Ḥusayn-`Alí Nuri** (Persian: میرزا حسینعلی نوری), was the founder of the Bahá'í Faith. He claimed to be the prophetic fulfilment of Bábism, a 19th-century outgrowth of Shí'ism, but in a broader sense claimed to be a messenger from God referring to the fulfilment of the eschatological expectations

---

[6] Monotheism at: http://en.wikipedia.org/wiki/Monotheism

of Islam, Christianity, and other major religions.[7]) in nineteenth-century Persia, emphasizing the spiritual unity of all humankind. There are an estimated five to six million Bahá'ís around the world in more than 200 countries and territories.

In the Bahá'í Faith, religious history is seen to have unfolded through a series of divine messengers, each of whom established a religion that was suited to the needs of the time and the capacity of the people. These messengers have included Abraham, Buddha(**Siddhārtha Gautama** (Sanskrit; Pali **Siddhattha Gotama**) was a spiritual teacher in the north eastern region of the Indian subcontinent who founded Buddhism. In most Buddhist traditions, he is regarded as the Supreme *Buddha* (Sammāsambuddha) of our age, "Buddha" meaning "awakened one" or "the enlightened one."[8]), Jesus, Muhamamad (**Muhammad ibn 'Abdullāh** (Arabic: محمد; Transliteration: *Muḥammad;* pronounced [muħammæd] (listen); also spelled **Mohammed** or **Muhammed**)[3][4][5] (ca. 570/571

---

[7] Bahá'u'lláh at: http://en.wikipedia.org/wiki/Bah%C3%A1%27u%27ll%C3%A1h

[8] Gautama Buddha at: http://en.wikipedia.org/wiki/Gautama_Buddha

The K.I.S.S. Principle

Mecca[مَكَّةَ]/[مَكَّهْ] – June 8, 632 Medina), is the founder of the religion of Islam [الإسْلام] and is regarded by Muslims as a messenger and prophet of God (Arabic: اللّٰه Allāh), the last and the greatest law-bearer in a series of Islamic prophets as taught by the Qur'an 33:40–40. Muslims thus consider him the restorer of an uncorrupted original monotheistic faith (*islām*) of Adam, Noah, Abraham, Moses, Jesus and other prophets. He was also active as a diplomat, merchant, philosopher, orator, legislator, reformer, military general, and, according to Muslim belief, an agent of divine action.[9]) and others, and most recently the Báb(**Siyyid `Alí Muḥammad Shírází** (Persian: سید علی محمد شیرازی) (October 20, 1819 – July 9, 1850) was the founder of Bábism, and one of three central figures of the Bahá'í Faith. He was a merchant from Shíráz, Persia, who at the age of twenty-four (on May 23, 1844) claimed to be the promised Qá'im (or Mahdi). After his declaration he took the title of **Báb** (Arabic: باب) meaning "Gate". He composed hundreds of letters and books (often termed *tablets*) in which he stated his messianic claims and defined his teachings, which constituted

---

[9] Muhammad at: http://en.wikipedia.org/wiki/Muhammad

a new *sharí'ah* or religious law. His movement eventually acquired tens of thousands of supporters, was virulently opposed by Iran's Shi'a clergy, and was suppressed by the Iranian government leading to thousands of his followers, termed Bábís, being persecuted and killed. In 1850 the Báb was shot by a firing squad in Tabríz aged thirty.[10]) and Bahá'u'lláh. In Bahá'í belief, each consecutive messenger prophesied of messengers to follow, and Bahá'u'lláh's life and teachings fulfilled the end-time promises of previous scriptures. Humanity is understood to be in a process of collective evolution, and the need of the present time is for the gradual establishment of peace, justice and unity on a global scale.[11]

Please note once again, according to the Baha'i Faith, that no matter what you believe is the way to get to God or his place of bliss, that the main messenger or prophet of your faith is on the same plain as the main messenger or prophet of any other belief and the God you believe in is the same person that every other belief or religious community believes in. You just have a different way to reach him.

---

[10] Báb at: http://en.wikipedia.org/wiki/The_B%C3%A1b

[11] Baha'I Faith at: http://en.wikipedia.org/wiki/Bahai#cite_note-0

The K.I.S.S. Principle

Salvation according to Scientology

This particular belief appears to be very peculiar and borders on the science fiction writings of it's founder, Ron L. Hubbard. It is not enough to provide a statement concerning what this belief actually sets forth as what most would call salvation. Therefore the following is provided in an effort, in short, to provide you with enough insight into their beliefs to enable you to understand what they believe bring them to the point of salvation...

> Scientology is a 20th Century religion that saw a gap in our society and tried to fill it. The Church was founded by L. Ron Hubbard (1911-1986) in 1954 after a successful career as a science fiction writer of the 1930s and 1940s. Hubbard changed his focus and his audience in founding the Church of Scientology. No longer was his main interest science fiction, but the paradigm shifted to philosophical and religious content that established one of the fastest growing religions among young and affluent people in our society during the last century. Second-generation Scientologists are on the rise, as children born to the early members have now matured to adulthood. Many of these people have not heard of the genuine gospel of Jesus Christ, which then, creates a new mission field in America and worldwide. Those

in Scientology need to hear the saving gospel message of Jesus...

One of the first principles taught to the Scientologist is that you are not your body. According to them, you are a Thetan. A Thetan is a spirit-being (similar to the soul) that has supposedly existed for some 300 trillion years. The Thetan is subject to reincarnation on this planet and other planets in the universe.

The problem for the Scientologist is that each past life had aberrations and painful experiences, called Engrams, which attached themselves to the Thetan, like barnacles to a ship. The presence of Engrams is what makes the individual react so overtly in society. Scientology's solution is to remove the Engrams from the Thetan.

The only provision for removing Engrams in Scientology is through "Auditing" and technical courses. These can become very costly, sometimes into the tens of thousands of dollars. Once the Engrams are totally removed, then the Thetan is pronounced "Clear," which produces two main benefits among others. The first is that the Clear Scientologist is an actualized Operating Thetan (OT), with control over Matter, Energy, Space, and

The K.I.S.S. Principle

> Time (MEST). Clear Scientologists can access total recall of their memory and takes charge of their MEST world. The second major benefit of being Clear is freedom from the endless cycle of birth and death (reincarnation)...
>
> Salvation, according to Scientology, is to be released from reincarnation, "... personal salvation in one lifetime [is] freedom from the cycle of birth and death [reincarnation]..."[12]

That being said, the view of salvation from the perspective of Scientology is to reach a point or place in their belief system where they have control, basically, over their existence and are placed in a status they call, 'Clear', or that is free from or released from the act of reincarnation..., which resembles, to some extent, Hinduism. This belief doesn't take them to a place of bliss elsewhere, but is concerned with making that place of bliss here, keeping them from returning in future lives. The question is, what happens to them, when they reach a status they call, 'Clear', and die?

---

[12] Challenging Scientology... at: http://www.invitation.to/dance/cults-scientology.htm

Salvation according to Atheists and Agnostics

At times, for those who do not understand the differences between Agnostics and Atheists, they assume that the two are the same. However, they are fundamentally different.

While an Atheist believes that God doesn't exist, an Agnostic basically believes that you can't know whether God does or doesn't exist:

> Atheism is characterized by an absence of belief in the existence of gods. This absence of belief generally comes about either through deliberate choice, or from an inherent inability to believe religious teachings which seem literally incredible. It is not a lack of belief born out of simple ignorance of religious teachings.

> Some atheists go beyond a mere absence of belief in gods: they actively believe that particular gods, or all gods, do not exist. Just lacking belief in Gods is often referred to as the "weak atheist" position; whereas believing that gods do not (or cannot) exist is known as "strong atheism."[13]

---

[13] What is atheism? at: http://www.infidels.org/library/modern/mathew/intro.html

The K.I.S.S. Principle

> The term 'agnosticism' was coined by Professor T.H. Huxley at a meeting of the Metaphysical Society in 1876. He defined an "<u>agnostic</u>" as someone who disclaimed both ("strong") atheism and theism, and who believed that the question of whether a higher power existed was unsolved and insoluble. Another way of putting it is that an agnostic is someone who believes that we do not know for sure whether God exists. Some agnostics believe that we can never know.[14]

So, according to the Atheist, who believe that God doesn't exist, then neither does salvation or gaining eternal bliss in a place called Heaven or the obvious alternative of being condemned to eternal punishment in a place called Hell. They are concerned only with the here and now. While on the other hand the Agnostic simply says that it is not possible to know whether these persons and/or places exist. Therefore, they too are concerned with the here and now.

For those that say they do not believe in God or those who say that it is not possible to know whether or not God exists, I would like to remind them that Atheism or the belief that God doesn't exist must be taught to them. It is a proven fact, worldwide, that

---

[14] What is agnosticism then? at: http://www.infidels.org/library/modern/mathew/intro.html

all enter this life with an inborn knowledge of God or that is a supreme being. Based on this, even those who claim to be Agnostic must be taught that they cannot know whether or not God exists. I will not go into detail concerning this fact here, but simply say that no matter where you go on our fair globe, whether deepest darkest Africa, the jungles of South America, etc., any place where so-called civilized man has never been, you will find people believing in God!

To this point, the focus has been on the religions of the world, apart from Christianity and their design on or their view of eternal salvation or how to attain eternal bliss. In each case, it has been found that a person belonging to the said belief must do good works in order to attain the level that will merit them eternal bliss, whether that place be here on earth or a place called heaven. And those whose beliefs either do not allow them to believe in God or that they can even know whether He exists believe that there place of bliss or torment is here on earth. So, they must make their best effort here to attain the highest level of happiness and/or bliss, because when they die, that's it. There isn't anything else!

PART II

MISCONCEPTIONS OF RELIGIOUS VARIANTS

In regard to distorted Christian so-called beliefs…

This chapter, as the title states, deals with Religious Variants. What is meant by this, is that while most, if not all, of the views set forth in this section state that they believe in Jesus Christ, they believe that He was a great man, prophet, teacher, etc., but may not believe that He was, in fact, God in the flesh. And those that do believe that He is God have a *skewed* view of His part in the salvation of man…

The K.I.S.S. Principle

Salvation according to Jehovah Witnesses

The Jehovah Witnesses have a view of Jesus Christ that confirms that He existed in human form and was a great teacher, prophet, etc., but is not God. Evidently, they believe that He is important to the salvation of man, but since He is not God, He couldn't make the payment for man's sin and thus provide him with eternal salvation. Their view of salvation can be seen in the following excerpt from their publication, the Watchtower:

> *You Can Live Forever in Paradise on Earth-But How?*
>
> 'LIVING forever on earth is just an impossible dream. There is no way anybody can do it.'
>
> You may have heard people say that. Yet you may know that in the beginning it was God's purpose for obedient humans to live forever in an earthly Paradise. And God never fails to accomplish what he purposes! (Genesis 1:28; Isaiah 55:11) His Word plainly promises: "The righteous themselves will possess the earth, and they will reside forever upon it."-Psalm 37:29.
>
> That is the thrilling message that Jehovah's Witnesses bring to people when they call at their homes. The

22

Kingdom, with Jesus Christ as Ruler, will see to it that God's original purpose is accomplished. Under the Kingdom's righteous administration this earth will be cultivated to become a beautiful Paradise. However, not everyone will be permitted to live in the Paradise earth. Requirements must be met. That is reasonable.-Matthew 6:10.

Consider: If you were the owner of a beautiful home surrounded by well-kept gardens, would you allow just anyone to live there? No, he would have to meet with your approval, meeting your requirements. What does God require of those who will reside forever upon his Paradise earth? Let us examine four basic requirements.

Four Requirements

1. Jesus Christ identified a first require-ment when he said in prayer to his Father: "This means everlasting life, their taking in knowledge of you, the only true God, and of the one whom you sent forth, Jesus Christ." (John 17:3) Knowledge of God and of Jesus Christ includes knowledge of God's purposes regarding the earth and of Christ's role as earth's new King. Will you take in such knowledge by studying the Bible?

The K.I.S.S. Principle

2. Many have found the <u>second require-</u><u>ment more difficult. It is to obey God's</u><u>laws</u>, yes, to conform one's life to the moral requirements set out in the Bible. This includes refraining from a debauched, immoral way of life.-<u>1</u><u>Corinthians 6:9</u>, <u>10</u>; <u>1 Peter 4:3</u>, <u>4</u>.

3. A <u>third requirement</u> is that we be associated with God's channel, his organization. God has always used an organization. For example, only those in the ark in Noah's day survived the Flood, and only those associated with the Christian congregation in the first century had God's favor. (<u>Acts 4:12</u>) Similarly, Jehovah is using only one organization today to accomplish his will. To receive everlasting life in the earthly Paradise we must identify that organization and serve God as part of it.

4. The <u>fourth requirement</u> is connected with loyalty. God requires that prospective subjects of his Kingdom support his government by loyally advocating his Kingdom rule to others. Jesus Christ explained: "This good news of the kingdom will be preached in all the inhabited earth." (<u>Matthew 24:14</u>) Will you meet this

> requirement by telling others about God's Kingdom?
>
> Perhaps you are well acquainted with these requirements. Yet many persons are ignorant of God's purposes and of what he requires. Now we have a marvelous instrument to help such ones. It is the book You Can Live Forever in Paradise on Earth. Have you used it to help others learn what God requires of them?[15]

Please note that this belief never points to the redemption of man through the shed blood of Christ on the cross of Calvary. It points to a works based relationship with their core beliefs and church that earns the person salvation, '...on earth.' The Jehovah Witnesses not only do not believe in a place of torment called Hell, but they also do not believe in a place of bliss called Heaven. They believe that when the body dies, the soul goes into a state of sleep, but that death may not be the end of everything, if God decides to resurrect the body...[16] In this, they appear to believe that death is a place of *non-existence*.

---

[15] "You Can Live Forever in Paradise on Earth-But How?" *Watchtower*, Feb. 15, 1983, page 12-13

[16] "What Happens When You Die?", Bible Questions Answered, at: http://www.jw.org/en/bible-teachings/questions/when-you-die/

The K.I.S.S. Principle

Salvation according to Mormons

The Church of Jesus Christ of the Latter Day Saints

The Mormons have a view of Jesus Christ as…and believe that Salvation is brought about not only by believing in the atoning payment of Christ on the cross, but that the individual is also responsible for repenting, being baptized, receiving the Holy Ghost and enduring in faith to the end in order to be saved. They say that this is the true doctrine of Christ:

> "True doctrines are always found in the Lord's true Church, because the channel of communication between God and His people is open" (Bruce R. McConkie, *Mormon Doctrine*, 2nd ed., 204). The truths of salvation include the teachings of the true scriptures, plus the principles of pure religion revealed directly from God to His prophets. The gospel has been restored in order to reestablish lost truths of the gospel and to confound false doctrine.

> "The true doctrine of Christ is that all men must come unto Him, gain faith, repent, be baptized, receive the Holy Ghost,

26

and endure in faith to the end in order to gain salvation" (McConkie, 204). [17]

This is revealed in points 3 and 4 of the Mormon "Articles of Faith", shown below:

The Articles of Faith of The Church of Jesus Christ of Latter-day Saints

<u>Joseph Smith the Prophet</u>

3 We believe that through the Atonement of Christ, all mankind may be saved, by obedience to the laws and ordinances of the Gospel.

4 We believe that the first principles and ordinances of the Gospel are: first, Faith in the Lord Jesus Christ; second, Repentance; third, Baptism by immersion for the remission of sins; fourth, Laying on of hands for the gift of the Holy Ghost. [18]

A deeper reading and understanding of Mormon beliefs reveals that every human being had a pre-existing form with God and the process of salvation takes the individual through physical birth, a time of testing on earth that incorporates a need to

---

[17] Mormon Doctrine of Salvation at: http://www.mormonbeliefs.org/mormon_beliefs/mormon-doctrine-salvation

[18] Articles of Faith at: http://www.mormonbeliefs.org/articles_faith

The K.I.S.S. Principle

have faith in God and follow His commandments, death(that is considered as a doorway into a new life), the spirit world, resurrection, and judgment that based upon their actions during mortality places them in one of four places:

The Steps of the Plan of Salvation

Pre-mortal Existence

Before a person is born into the mortal world (earth-life) he lived with Heavenly Father. All people are His children. They learned, formed relationships, and developed talents in the pre-mortal existence. However, they could only progress so far, so Heavenly Father presented them with a way to become more like Him.

Birth

Those who chose to follow Heavenly Father's plan in the pre-mortal life have been or will be born. Birth is the way they gain physical bodies, and is an important step in the plan of salvation.

Mortality

This time on earth is like a test. Everyone needs to learn how to have faith in God and follow His commandments. People

Creation and Fall

According to Mormonism these were necessary steps. The Fall is actually a positive event that provides the necessary mortal experience which is needed to become like God.

Death

Like birth, death is a doorway into a new life. Through death people again enter the Spirit world.

Spirit World

In the spirit world there will be two conditions of existence, spirit prison; for those who did not have the opportunity to learn the gospel of Christ or who rejected it, and spirit paradise, for the righteous. Those in spirit prison will have the opportunity to learn about and accept the gospel.

The term "spirit prison" does not have the same connotation as a "prison" on earth, but only means that a spirit in that condition cannot advance in light, knowledge and preparation for eternity

The K.I.S.S. Principle

until he receives the covenants of the gospel of Christ. Those who performed good works and did not commit major sins while living by the light and knowledge that they had, will rest from care and sorrow but will still need to progress, hence their condition can be described as a spirit prison, but it is a good place. The wicked, however, will suffer in spirit prison, though they will still have an opportunity to hear the plan of repentance, <u>forgiveness</u>, and salvation through Jesus Christ.

Resurrection

This is the reuniting of the body and spirit. Every person who has ever lived will be resurrected.

Judgment

After resurrection, men are brought before the judgment bar of Christ. All will be judged for their actions during mortality. Each person will be put into one of four places based on his actions: the Celestial (highest) kingdom, Terrestrial kingdom, Telestial kingdom, Outer

Darkness (equivalent of Hell, only a few will be sent here). [19]

Salvation according to Seventh Day Adventism

Seventh Day Adventism professes to hold to the same doctrinal beliefs of mainstream Protestant Beliefs, yet while they profess a belief in Jesus Christ as God's Son, the redeemer of mankind through His payment for sin on the cross of Calvary, they also apparently believe that a so-called saved individual **will** be obedient to keeping the law of God indicating that if they don't, they are not really saved...

> While asserting that Christians are saved entirely by the grace of God, Adventists also stress obedience to the law of God as the proper response to salvation. [20]

This seems to place emphasis on the fact that in order to be saved or at least appear saved, a person is required to not only accept the payment that Christ made for them on the cross, but to also follow or that is be obedient to the law. This is adding something to the payment for sin that Christ made and seems to say that His payment

---

[19] The Steps of the Plan of Salvation at: http://www.mormonwiki.com/Plan_of_Salvation

[20] Soteriology and free will at: http://en.wikipedia.org/wiki/Seventh-day_Adventist_teaching#Soteriology

The K.I.S.S. Principle

wasn't enough. This would also appear to remove God's need to discipline His Child, in accord with Hebrews 12:6,12, because according to their belief, if the individual wasn't being obedient to God, they would not be His Child!

Salvation according to Christian Science and Unity

Christian Science

Christian Science was the outgrowth of a young woman named Mary Baker Glover Patterson Eddy, who was very unsettled by the doctrine of unconditional election or predestination as taught by the Congregationalist church her parents belonged to. She was greatly troubled by this teaching and unwilling to be *saved*, if her siblings were numbered with those who were doomed. She discovered what is called the Principals of Christian Science in 1866 after a serious fall brought her near death. As with other divergent beliefs, Christian Science claims further revelation that goes beyond the Bible or in other words truth that was previously unrevealed. This brings us to the Christian Science view of salvation which is connected to its overall belief that there is no such thing as sin and thus salvation is totally unnecessary:

> Concerning salvation, Mrs. Eddy said: "Life, Truth, and Love understood and demonstrated as supreme over all; sin,

Rev. Clayton Hampton

sickness and death destroyed" *(Science and Health, p.* 593:2022). Since to the Christian Scientist there is no such thing as sin, salvation in the biblical sense is totally unnecessary. The teachings concerning salvation in Mrs. Eddy's writings are both ambiguous and inconsistent. She stated over and over again that sin is just an illusion *(Miscellaneous Writings,* 27:1112, *Science and Health,* 71:2, 287:22, 23, 480:23, 24, etc.).

On the other hand, she states as quoted above, that salvation is sin, sickness and death destroyed." If sin is only an illusion, having no real existence, how can it be destroyed? Putting it another way, do you destroy something that does not exist? Since there is no harmonious teaching in Christian Science concerning salvation, it is difficult to evaluate it objectively. Nevertheless, the Christian Science view is a far cry from the Bible that teaches the reality of sin (Romans 3:23) and the need for a Savior (Acts 4:12).[21]

It is apparent that since the founder had a problem with the doctrine of Salvation as taught in the Bible that she was enlightened with a new revelation

---

[21] Christian Science:Salvation at: http://www.greatcom.org/resources/handbook_of_todays_religions/01chap11/default.htm

from God that sets forth the belief that sin is an illusion. And since sin is an illusion, then there is no need for salvation from something that can't be destroyed.

Unity

Unity was founded in 1889 with roots in Christian Science. The Unity School of Christianity began as a quest for physical healing by its co-founder, Mary Caroline Page, known as Myrtle, the wife of Charles Fillmore. While the Fillmores were both students of a mental healer and metaphysician named Phineas Parkhurst Quimby, Myrtle had been a follower of Mary Baker Eddy, the founder of Christian Science. So, while both were influenced by Quimby, their beliefs were rooted in Christian Science.

> The ultimate goal of those who follow Unity teaching is to recognize their "oneness" with the "Force," thereby realizing their true self, the God-Self. The god of Unity is an adaptation of Hindu belief regarding the divine. God is a part of His creation. God is in all things...

However, many of Unity's beliefs are based upon not only Christian Science doctrine, but eastern religions as in their beliefs concerning salvation:

> H. Emilie Cady in her book, *Lessons in Truth*, says that "man originally lived

consciously in the spiritual part of himself. He fell by descending in his consciousness to the external or more material part of himself." In other words, the fall of man was from the spiritual realm to the physical and this fall has caused him to suffer spiritual amnesia. Therefore man's dilemma is to reclaim his place in the spiritual realm through right thinking.

Unity teaches that as man discovers his innate divinity he continues to raise his consciousness until he becomes fully God- realized. Once man has achieved this state of understanding he recognizes that he is in perfect oneness with God and is not in need of redemption but that he is indeed the divine.

The unbiblical position regarding salvation held by Unity is clearly seen in the Unity publication, *The Way to Salvation*. This pamphlet states that "Jesus Christ was not meant to be slain as a substitute for man; that is, to atone vicariously for him. Each person must achieve at-one-ment with God, by letting the Christ Spirit within him resurrect his soul into Christ perfection."

Curtis says that "more than ever, we need to become quiet and focus upon

The K.I.S.S. Principle

> the inner. We need to be still and to know that the presence within is God." When one becomes fully aware of this divine presence salvation is realized because the individual no longer has a sense of lostness.[22]

So, according to Unity, all a person need do to obtain salvation is to become fully aware of the presence within as being God.

Salvation according to the Children of God

The Family / The Family International

It would be very easy to get involved in a discussion concerning the apparent faults, or discrepancies of this group as well as many of their beliefs that are an outright contradiction of scripture. However, this section of this communication is dedicated to revealing the view of *The Children of God* concerning salvation or their presentation of salvation.

To properly evaluate the message of this group, we should probably go back to its inception in 1968. The group was founded by David Berg as an outgrowth of his disenchantment with organized religion[23], with respect to properly fulfilling the Great Commission. He felt that organized

---

[22] Unity:Salvation at: http://www.leaderu.com/orgs/probe/docs/unity.html

[23] David Berg: Disenchantment with Organized Religion, at: http://www.davidberg.org/mission/disenchantment-with-organized-religion

religion was more focused on building projects for the local body, other issues internal to their local body, becoming a status symbol, being more of a social club, etc. than focusing on God's command to 'Go' and reach the world with the Gospel of Christ. The group has grown from a small body in 1968 to an international organization now known as 'The Family International'. His view originally appeared to not only be heartfelt, and genuine, but Bible based. His view of salvation, at that point in time was a simple trusting in Christ as Savior.

> We know that our Salvation doesn't depend on our going to church on Sunday! It depends on our trusting Jesus Christ as our Savior![24]

His stated concern for getting this message out is apparent in his statement,

> The main thing I care about is getting out the Gospel, getting God's message of Love to the lost, to the people who need it, to liberate the captives, save the lost, heal the sick and preach the Gospel to the whole world![25]

---

[24] David Berg: Disenchantment with Organized Religion, at: http://www.davidberg.org/mission/disenchantment-with-organized-religion

[25] David Berg: The Gospel Message, at: http://www.davidberg.org/mission/the-gospel-message

The K.I.S.S. Principle

And, according to the doctrinal beliefs currently held to by *The Family International*, apparently they still hold to this core belief,

Salvation by Grace

We believe that God created the first man and woman without sin. He granted them free choice, and they fell into sin through their choice to disobey God. Through this entrance of sin into the world, all people became sinners by nature (Romans 5:12–14) and separated from God. But God, in His infinite love and mercy, reconciled humanity to Himself by giving the world His only Son, "that whoever believes in Him should not perish, but have everlasting life" (John 3:16). We believe, therefore, that anyone who accepts God's pardon for sin through Jesus Christ will be forgiven and redeemed and will live forever in God's presence in the afterlife.

Salvation (redemption from sin) is a gift of God's love, mercy, and forgiveness, and can only be attained through belief in Jesus. "Not by works of righteousness which we have done, but according to His mercy He saved us" (Titus 3:5). Having received the gift of salvation, the believer is saved forever; after death, his or her soul will live

Rev. Clayton Hampton

forever in Heaven. "I give them eternal life, and they shall never perish; neither shall anyone snatch them out of My hand" (John 10:28). Believers continue to be fallible people in need of God's forgiveness, but despite their shortcomings and sins, they will never lose their salvation.

Genesis 3:17–19; 1 Corinthians 15:21–22; Romans 3:23, 6:23; Ephesians 2:7–9; 1 John 1:8; Acts 4:12; 1 John 5:12; Romans 5:8–9, 8:38–39[26]

It is the opinion of this writer that it is a real shame that a group such as this could be so apparently clear on the message of salvation and so unscriptural in the practice of many of their other so called Biblical/Christian beliefs. I believe that their unscriptural practices in other areas cause many to reject their apparent clear presentation of God's plan for redemption.

Salvation according to Sun Myung Moon

The Unification Church

Sun Myung Moon founded The Unification Church in 1954, believing that he is the Messiah of the

---

[26] The Family International: Salvation by Grace, at: http://www.thefamily-international.org/en/about/our-beliefs/salvation-grace/

The K.I.S.S. Principle

Second Coming and that his family is the first true family in all history!

> He claims that in 1936, when he was 16, Jesus Christ appeared to him on a mountainside in Northwestern Korea and told him that God had chosen him for the mission of establishing the Kingdom of Heaven on Earth. After World War II, Moon returned to Pyongyang, the capital of communist North Korea, where he set up his first church (1945)...

There are many questionable beliefs that Moon has given his followers, the one we are concerned with here is Salvation:

> Moonies teach the "Law of Indemnity" -- that God's children must pay for at least a part of their debt of sin before God will forgive them. They believe a person earns his salvation through fasting, fund-raising, recruitment, and other such works. They claim that both a spiritual and a physical salvation are needed -- and that the "third Adam" will provide physical salvation by marrying and producing sinless children (*Divine Principle*, p. 148). They teach that once the "third Adam" comes, those who have paid indemnity will also be able to marry and bear sinless children. Moonies view Moon as that "third Adam" who provides

> physical salvation through a perfect
> family (indeed, his twelve children are
> considered sinless!), and extends this
> perfection to his followers through their
> obedience to him.[27]

Please note that apart from all of the other beliefs of this so-called religion, that the doctrinal position they hold is works based. In other words, the payment that Christ made on the cross isn't enough. Man is required to '...pay for at least a part of their debt of sin before God will forgive him.'

Salvation according to Judaism

You may be wondering why Judaism has been placed in this particular section of this book. While historic Judaism is the predecessor of modern day Christianity, modern day Judaism not only didn't follow the path or teachings of historic Judaism and trust in Christ as the promised Messiah foretold by their prophets, but have even changed their belief in a coming personal Messiah to that of a Messianic Period. Therefore, their beliefs are not only a far cry from where it came from, but also far from when their belief was intended to take them:

> Judaism, while admitting the exis-
> tence of sin, its abhorrence by God,
> and the necessity for atonement, has

---

[27] Sun Myung Moon:Salvation at: http://www.rapidnet.com/%7Ejbeard/bdm/exposes/moon/general.htm

The K.I.S.S. Principle

not developed a system of salvation teaching as found in Christianity. Atonement is accomplished by sacrifices, penitence, good deeds and a little of God's grace. No concept of substitutionary atonement (as in Christianity in the Person of Jesus Christ)exists.

Scholar Michael Wyschogrod explains the difference:

A Jew who believes that man is justified by works of the law would hold the belief that man can demand only strict justice from God, nothing more. Such a man would say to God: "Give me what I deserve, neither more nor less; I do not need your mercy, only your strict justice."

If there are Jews who approach God in this spirit, I have never met nor heard of them. In the morning liturgy that Jews recite daily, we find the following:

"Master of all worlds: It is not on account of our own righteousness that we offer our supplications before thee, but on account of thy great compassion. What are we? What is our life? What is our goodness? What is our virtue? What is our help? What our strength? What our might?"

Rev. Clayton Hampton

The believing Jew is fully aware that if he were to be judged strictly according to his deeds by the standards of justice and without mercy he would be doomed. He realizes that without the mercy of God there is no hope for him and that he is therefore justified -if by "justified" we mean that he avoids the direst of divine punishments -not by the merit of his works as commanded in the Torah, but by the gratuitous mercy of God who saves man in spite of the fact that man does not deserve it (Tanenbaum, Wilson, and Rudin, eds., Evangelicals and Jews in Conversation on Scripture, Theology, and History, Grand Rapids, ME Baker Book House, 1978, pp. 47, 48).

So then, Jews do believe in the mercy of God but they do not believe in any sub-stitutionary atonement that once and for all time cleanses them from all sin. Contrast this with the great passage of assurance in Hebrews 7:22-28 (NASB):

So much the more also Jesus has become the guarantee of a better cov-enant. And the former priests, on the one hand, existed in greater numbers, because they were prevented by death from continuing, but He, on the other hand, because He abides forever, holds His priesthood permanently. Hence,

The K.I.S.S. Principle

also, He is able to save forever those who draw near to God through Him, since He always lives to make intercession for them. For it was fitting that we should have such a high priest, holy, innocent, undefiled, separated from sinners and exalted above the heavens; who does not need daily, like those high priests, to offer up sacrifices, first for His own sins, and then for the sins of the people, because this He did once for all when He offered up Himself. For the Law appoints men as high priests who are weak, but the work of the oath, which came after the Law, appoints a Son, made perfect forever.[28]

As you can see from the previous information, while today's Jews may acknowledge the existence of sin due to God's abhorrence of it, and therefore a need for an atonement for it, they have no actual valid payment for it. For if they believe, as many do, that they either or should be justified by their works, then they are doomed. In fact, I find it very interesting that Jewish history reveals:

In the course of Jewish history the meaning of the Messiah had undergone changes. Originally it was believed that God would send His special messenger,

---

[28] Salvation in Judaism at: http://www.greatcom.org/resources/handbook_of_todays_religions/03chap08/default.htm

delivering Israel from her oppressors and instituting peace and freedom. However, today, any idea of a personal messiah has been all but abandoned by the majority of Jews. It has been substituted with the hope of a messianic age characterized by truth and justice.

Within the history of Judaism, from the time of Jesus of Nazareth until Moses Hayyim Luzatto (died A.D. 1747), there have been at least 34 different prominent Jews who have claimed to be the Messiah (James Hastings, Encyclopedia of Religion and Ethics, Vol. 8, New York and London: Scribner's and T & T Clark, 1919, pp. 581-588).[29]

This writer finds it very interesting that the Jews appear to have accepted all but one of the acclaimed Messiahs. The one they rejected, they nailed to a tree.

Salvation according to Unitarians

Unitarianism is a religion based on belief in God as a single unitary being, as opposed to the Christian belief in a Triune God, existent in Father, Son, and Holy Ghost. They believe that man is basically good and thus has no need of salvation:

---

[29] Doctrine Judaism and the Messiah at: http://www.greatcom.org/resources/handbook_of_todays_religions/03chap08/default.htm

The K.I.S.S. Principle

...Unitarian Universalists see no essential need for the traditional concepts of Christian redemption and salvation. Since men are not sinners, they do not need forgiveness from sin.

For them, salvation—for lack of a better word—is simply an individual's achievement of self-actualization. In this view, whatever way one finds meaning or purpose for her life is valid.

> "For us, salvation is not an otherworldly journey, flown on wings of dogma. It is ethical striving and moral growth: respect for the personalities and experiences of others; faith in human dignity and potentiality; aversion to sanctimony and bigotry; reverence for the gift of life; confidence in a true harmony of mind and spirit, of nature and human nature; faith in the ability to give and receive love; and a quest for broad, encompassing religious expression-spiritual yet practical, personal and communal."

(Jack Mendelsohn, *Being Liberal in An Illiberal Age*)[30]

This belief can be traced as far back as A.D. 256-336 and the teachings of Arius, a pastor in Alexandria, Egypt. He taught that Jesus, the son was created and thus not equal to God the Father. Their way of salvation is basically based upon the here and now and how a person can better their life and or existence.

Salvation according to the Masons

First of all, it may be a good idea to describe or define who the Masons are. According to Joseph Fort Newton in his book, The Builders, he advises that while several definitions of Masonry have been given, that the best description is provided by the German, *Handbuch*:

> Masonry is the activity of closely united men who, employing symbolical forms borrowed principally from the mason's trade and from architecture, work for the welfare of mankind, striving morally to ennoble themselves and others, and thereby to bring about a universal

---

[30] Salvation is finding one's own self-fulfillment and truth at: http://www.4truth.net/site/c.hiKXLbPNLrF/b.2950167/k.7244/Unitarian_Universalists.htm

The K.I.S.S. Principle

league of mankind, which they aspire
to exhibit even now on a small scale.[31]

At best, this reveals that the Masons are a works based organization, apparently working for '...*a universal league of mankind.*' Newton goes on to say:

> ...of no one religion, it finds great truths in all religions.
>
> High above all dogmas that divide, all bigotries that blind, all bitterness that beclouds, will be written the simple words of the one eternal religion—the Fatherhood of God, the brotherhood of man, the moral law, the golden rule, and the hope of a life everlasting![32]

While the Masons claim that they are not a religious organization, the statement by Wm. Hutchinson regarding the organization's acceptance of men of various faiths states:

> ...All Masons, therefore whether Christians, Jews, or Mohammedans, who violate not the rule of right, written by the Almighty upon the tables of the heart, who Do fear Him, and WORK

---

[31] Vol. I, p. 320. The *Handbuch* si an encyclopedia of Masonry, published in 1900. See admirable review of it, *A. Q. C.*, xi, 65.

[32] The Builders, Part III, Chapter I, What it Masonry at: http://www.freemasons-freemasonry.com/Newton_builders_fr.html

righteousness, we are to acknowledge as brethren; and, though we take different roads, we are not to be angry with, or persecute each other on that account. We mean to travel to the same place; we know that the end of our journey is the same; and we affectionately hope to meet in the Lodge of perfect happiness.[33]

If this statement is, in fact, true as to what the Masons believe and teach, then their beliefs are very close to that of the Bahai Faith. In other words, they would be teaching that though we may have different beliefs in who God is and or how to get to Him or Heaven, that we are all going to or end up in the same place!

This writer finds it oddly pointed out in Mr. Newton's book, that has been referenced several times here that:

Upon the altar of Masonry lies the open Bible which, despite the changes and advances of the ages, remains the greatest Modern Book—the moral manual of civilization.[34]

---

[33] The Builders, Part III, Chapter I, What it Masonry, quote by Wm. Hutchinson at: http://www.freemasons-freemasonry.com/Newton_builders_fr.html

[34] The Builders, Part III, Chapter I, What it Masonry at: http://www.freemasons-freemasonry.com/Newton_builders_fr.html

The K.I.S.S. Principle

The apparent conflict here lies between what they are teaching, and what the symbol of the open Bible teaches. For according to the scriptures laying open on their altar of Masonry state:

> I am the way, the truth, and the life. No man cometh to the Father, but by me.
>
> ~ John 14:6
>
> Neither is there salvation in any other: for there is none other name under heaven given among men, whereby we must be saved.
>
> ~ Acts 4:12

What is really amazing about this evaluation of the Masons is that Joseph Fort Newton, the author of the book, providing most of the information here, not only was a Grand Chaplin, but also a Baptist Minister! That being said, I do not understand how Baptist Beliefs on Salvation can be merged together with the Masonic Beliefs stated above. It would appear that a Baptist Minister would have a great deal of difficulty in not only agreeing with the Masonic Beliefs, but of even being a part of the organization, much less a Grand Chaplin.

PART III

MISCONCEPTIONS OF CHRISTENDOM

In regard to Christian beliefs…

The main thing that sets Christianity apart from ALL of the religions of the world is simply the resurrection of Jesus Christ. There is no belief on earth that makes such a claim *and backs up the set forth claim* with undeniable proof as does Christianity. In this, *most all* Christians are united. However, once you get past this point, differences between the various divisions become more evident, especially regarding salvation.

In Part I(Salvation according to the Baha'i Faith), the statement was made that the Baha'i Faith's view of salvation was the most puzzling. Why? I said that, because it is basically the same view that we

The K.I.S.S. Principle

in Christendom have of obtaining Salvation or that is Eternal Life with regard to all of the various divisions in Christendom. What I mean by that statement is that many in Christendom believe that no matter whether Catholic, or one of the Protestant Denominations or varied Christian Organizations, that all plans of salvation lead to the same place. However, while the desire of all is to do just that, the fact is that most of the plans of salvation set forth by the various divisions of Christianity lead us down a cloudy contradictory path that allows us to stray '…from the simplicity that is in Christ.' The fact is that many people are saved, not *because* of what is shared by well meaning or good intended Christians, but in *spite* of what is shared.

<u>Christian Divisions</u>
<u>Catholicism</u>
Salvation according to Catholic Church

Martin Luther's efforts to set forth the scriptural belief that salvation is not from good works, but a free gift of God, received only by grace through faith in Jesus as redeemer from sin in his '*Ninety-Five Thesis*', not only got him into trouble with the Catholic Church, but coupled with his refusal to retract all of his writings at the demand of Pope Leo X and the Holy Roman Emperor Charles V resulted in his excommunication by the pope and his condemnation as an outlaw by the emperor. Yet, that's not all, for his stand, in part, fueled the cause for the '*Council of Trent*'. The church sensed the need to answer what they considered the heretical teachings of Luther and those considered 'Protestants'. The information below encapsulates the teachings of Catholicism on salvation that came forth out of that Council...

> The Council of Trent describes the process of salvation from sin in the case of an adult with great minuteness (Sess. VI, v-vi).
>
> It begins with the *grace of God* which touches a sinner's heart, and calls him to repentance. This grace cannot be merited; it proceeds solely from the love and mercy of God. Man may receive or reject this inspiration of God, he may turn to God or remain in sin. Grace does not constrain man's free will.
>
> Thus assisted the sinner is *disposed for salvation* from sin; he believes in the revelation and promises of God, he fears God's justice, hopes in his mercy, trusts that God will be merciful to him for Christ's sake, begins to love God as the source of all justice, hates and detests his sins.
>
> This disposition is followed by *justification* itself, which consists not in the mere remission of sins, but in the sanctification and renewal of the inner man by the voluntary reception of God's grace

The K.I.S.S. Principle

and <u>gifts</u>, whence a man becomes just instead of <u>unjust</u>, a friend instead of a foe and so an heir according to hope of eternal life. This change happens either by reason of a perfect act of charity elicited by a well disposed sinner or by virtue of the Sacrament either of Baptism or of Penance according to the condition of the respective subject laden with <u>sin</u>. The Council further indicates the causes of this change. By the merit of the Most Holy Passion through the Holy Spirit, the charity of <u>God</u> is shed abroad in the hearts of those who are justified.

Against the <u>heretical</u> tenets of various times and <u>sects</u> we must hold

that the initial grace is truly gratuitous and <u>supernatural</u>;

- that the human will remains free under the influence of this grace;

- that man really cooperates in his personal salvation from <u>sin</u>;

- that by justification man is really made just, and not merely declared or reputed so;

Rev. Clayton Hampton

- that justification and sanctification are only two aspects of the same thing, and not <u>ontologically</u> and chronologically distinct realities;

- that justification excludes all mortal <u>sin</u> from the <u>soul</u>, so that the just man is no way liable to the sentence of <u>death</u> at <u>God's</u> judgment-seat.

- Other points involved in the foregoing process of personal salvation from <u>sin</u> are matters of discussion among <u>Catholic</u> <u>theologians</u>; such are, for instance,

the precise nature of initial grace,

- the manner in which grace and <u>free will</u> work together,

- the precise nature of the fear and the <u>love</u> disposing the sinner for justification,

- the manner in which <u>sacraments</u> cause <u>sanctifying grace</u>.

- But these questions are treated in other articles dealing *ex professo* with the respective subjects. The same is <u>true</u> of <u>final perseverance</u>

The K.I.S.S. Principle

> without which personal salvation from <u>sin</u> is not permanently secured.
>
> What has been said applies to the salvation of adults; children and those permanently deprived of their use of <u>reason</u> are saved by the <u>Sacrament of Baptism</u>. [35]

According to the information referenced above, it is revealed that they do not believe in the security of the believer or as stated in many Protestant beliefs, 'Once saved always saved'. The importance of this is that it is a confirmation that Catholicism does not believe that Christ's death payment for sin on the cross was a complete payment. It indicates whether by a direct statement or by inference that in order for a person to obtain salvation, they need to not only accept Christ's payment, but also include something else added to or to be included with Christ's payment to merit salvation. Not only that, but it goes further to state that without '*final perseverance…*' that '*…personal salvation from <u>sin</u> is not permanently secured.* ', which simply means that it(personal salvation) can be lost. Then, a closing statement is made stating that '*children and those permanently deprived of their use of reason are saved by the 'Sacrament of Baptism'*. I believe that I'd want to know what happens to a child that isn't baptized? To put this in plain language, Catholicism teaches that you can

---

[35] Individual Salvation at: <u>http://www.newadvent.org/cathen/13407a.htm</u>

Rev. Clayton Hampton

gain eternal life by trusting in Christ and following whatever their other guidelines are for attaining eternal life and then you can lose it, if you don't persevere and that anyone without the capability to reason can gain eternal life by being baptized. This is extremely unfortunate, for there is no basis for either teaching anywhere in scripture.

<u>Protestantism</u>
<u>Theological Beliefs</u>
Salvation according to Calvinism

Calvinistic teaching and/or doctrine is the product of its founder John Calvin, who although he grew up under the teachings of Roman Catholicism distanced himself from the Roman Catholic Church in 1536. He studied on his own, preached and played a major role in the Reformation movement of that time and is well known as a French reformer and theologian. While having composed many commentaries on the Bible, he may well be most remembered by 'The Five Points of Calvinism' easily remembered by the acrostic **TULIP**.

T

Total Depravity (Total Inability)

Total Depravity is probably the most misunderstood tenet of Calvinism. When Calvinists speak of humans as "totally depraved," they are making an extensive, rather than an intensive

The K.I.S.S. Principle

statement. The effect of the fall upon man is that sin has extended to every part of his personality -- his thinking, his emotions, and his will. Not necessarily that he is *intensely* sinful, but that sin has *extended* to his entire being.

The unregenerate (unsaved) man is dead in his sins (Romans 5:12). Without the power of the Holy Spirit, the natural man is blind and deaf to the message of the gospel (Mark 4:11f). This is why Total Depravity has also been called "Total Inability." The man without a knowledge of God will never come to this knowledge without God's making him alive through Christ (Ephesians 2:1-5).

U

Unconditional Election

Unconditional Election is the doctrine which states that God chose those whom he was pleased to bring to a knowledge of himself, not based upon any merit shown by the object of his grace and not based upon his looking forward to discover who would "accept" the offer of the gospel. God has elected, based solely upon the counsel of his own will, some for glory and others for damnation (Romans 9:15,21). He has done this act before the foundations of the world (Ephesians 1:4-8).

This doctrine does not rule out, however, man's responsibility to believe in the redeeming work of God the Son (John 3:16-18). Scripture presents a tension between God's sovereignty in salvation, and man's responsibility to believe which it does not try to resolve. Both are true -- to deny man's responsibility is to affirm an unbiblical hyper-calvinism; to deny God's sovereignty is to affirm an unbiblical Armenianism.

The elect are saved unto good works (Ephesians 2:10). Thus, though good works will never bridge the gulf between man and God that was formed in the Fall, good works are a result of God's saving grace. This is what Peter means when he admonishes the Christian reader to make his "calling" and "election" sure (2 Peter 1:10). Bearing the fruit of good works is an indication that God has sown seeds of grace in fertile soil.

L

Limited Atonement (Particular Redemption)

The K.I.S.S. Principle

Limited Atonement is a doctrine offered in answer to the question, "for whose sins did Christ atone?" The Bible teaches that Christ died for those whom God gave him to save (John 17:9). Christ died, indeed, for many people, but not all (Matthew 26:28). Specifically, Christ died for the invisible Church -- the sum total of all those who would ever rightly bear the name "Christian" (Ephesians 5:25).

This doctrine often finds many objections, mostly from those who think that Limited Atonement does damage to evangelism. We have already seen that Christ will not lose any that the father has given to him (John 6:37). Christ's death was not a death of potential atonement for all people. Believing that Jesus' death was a potential, symbolic atonement for anyone who might possibly, in the future, accept him trivializes Christ's act of atonement. Christ died to atone for specific sins of specific sinners. Christ died to make holy the church. He did not atone for all men, because obviously all men are not saved. Evangelism is actually lifted up in this doctrine, for the evangelist may tell his congregation that Christ died for sinners, and that he will not lose any of those for whom he died!

I

Irresistible Grace

The result of God's Irresistible Grace is the certain response by the elect to the inward call of the Holy Spirit, when the outward call is given by the evangelist or minister of the Word of God. Christ, himself, teaches that all whom God has elected will come to a knowledge of him (John 6:37). Men come to Christ in salvation when the Father calls them (John 6:44), and the very Spirit of God leads God's beloved to repentance (Romans 8:14). What a comfort it is to know that the gospel of Christ will penetrate our hard, sinful hearts and wondrously save us through the gracious inward call of the Holy Spirit (I Peter 5:10)!

P

Perseverance of the Saints

Perseverance of the Saints is a doctrine which states that the saints (those whom God has saved) will remain in God's hand until they are glorified and brought to abide with him in heaven. Romans 8:28-39 makes it clear that when a person truly has been regenerated by God, he will remain in God's

The K.I.S.S. Principle

> stead. The work of sanctification which God has brought about in his elect will continue until it reaches its fulfillment in eternal life (Phil. 1:6). Christ assures the elect that he will not lose them and that they will be glorified at the "last day" (John 6:39). The Calvinist stands upon the Word of God and trusts in Christ's promise that he will perfectly fulfill the will of the Father in saving all the elect.[36]

Basically, this is a belief based upon the composition of five doctrines that state that man is a sinner and that those whom God was pleased to bring to a knowledge of himself, He unconditionally elected to salvation. Following this line, Christ only died for those whom God unconditionally elected. It then follows that God's Grace is Irresistible to them who have been elected to salvation. Apparently, they have no choice, but to be saved and according to the last point in the list, they can't lose what God has given them by saving them to eternal life. The compilation of these doctrines postulate that God selects specific individuals to go to Heaven and specific individuals to go to Hell, based upon His Sovereignty and that *they have no choice* in the matter. But, the argument set forth is weak at best and causes the individual to either discount other clear scriptures that teach the opposite of this doctrine or to twist the scripture being viewed

---

[36] The Five Points of Calvinism at: http://www.reformed.org/calvinism/index.html

to fall in line or accommodate their doctrine. Take a quick look at:

> ...And I, if I be lifted up from the earth, will *draw all men* unto me.

> ~ John 12:32

This passage or statement was made by Jesus himself and indicates the He will *draw all* men to himself.

> *draw*(GK: **ἕλκω** - he'l-kō) means to draw by inward power, lead

> *all*(GK: **πᾶς** - pä's) means each, every, any, all, the whole, everyone

Note that the passage does not say *all elected* men or *all selected* men or *all chosen* men. The Greek definition of the word *all* indicates that the lifting up of Christ on the cross in a payment for sin(*all*) provides a drawing power within *all*, because *all* sin was paid for *all* men.

Also, the set forth doctrine proposes that God is selective in the process of His choosing individuals to go to Heaven or Hell, but it is plainly stated in His Word:

> ...For there is no *respect of persons* with God.

The K.I.S.S. Principle

~ Romans 2:11

The whole idea of this belief concerning salvation uses an unscriptural or perverted view of *Predestination* to prove their doctrine. But, the book of Ephesians is very clear on *Predestination*, which is bound up in one phrase that is seen throughout the book, "in Him" or "in Christ", etc. To set forth the idea that God can choose us and we can't choose Him is just not true.

> When we(my wife and I) went to Boston the first time for me to preach at a church on Cape Cod, we bought tickets for a flight from Atlanta to Boston. Delta Airlines had predetermined that they had a flight from Atlanta to Boston. But, it was our decision as to whether or not we wanted to be on that flight.

The fact is that God(according to Ephesians) has chosen all those who are "in Christ" to go to Heaven confirms the fact that He chose the way(Christ-John 14:6). And, we have the option of choosing whether or not we want to be "in Christ". God didn't create us as robots, but as separate entities, made like Him, made to have fellowship with Him, but with the ability to choose or reject Him.

All of that being said, if John Calvin was correct in his interpretation and/or assessment of salvation, then why would the Lord wait some 1500 years to provide enlightenment to someone(like him) concerning it? And, why would anyone want to believe in a teaching that didn't come around until some 1500 years after the original words of the Lord were given concerning salvation, etc.? Not only does this not make sense, but it makes the Lord into a very peculiar selector of persons, as well as not very organized and an unloving God(not giving an adequate answer to everyone from the time of the cross), when He clearly states that He is not a '...*respecter of persons.*' The line of belief taught by the acrostic *TULIP* changes the God of Love and Grace into an unloving, very selective, arrogant liar.

Salvation according to Armenianism

The Armenian view of salvation differs from Calvinism in more than one way, as shown below:

Arminian Five Points of the Remonstrance of 1610 with contrasting Five Points of Calvinism

1) **Election is conditioned upon man's response or <u>foreseen faith</u> (conditional "election")**

The Reformed Tradition, by contrast, teaches that election is <u>unconditional</u>.

2) **Universal Atonement** (According to Armenians Christ has already atoned and propitiated for the sins of all

The K.I.S.S. Principle

humanity. Christ purchased redemption not only for those who would believe but for all men, yet only those who believe go to heaven). The Reformed Tradition asks, if this is the case, why aren't all men saved if all their sins are atoned for? Unbelief is also a sin. By contrast, we believe the Bible teaches that the redemptive blessings of the atonement were intended only for those who would believe, the elect (<u>particular redemption</u>). Christ died in a way for the elect that He did not for the non-elect.

3) **"Unaided by the Holy Spirit, no person is able to respond to God's will"** (thus eliminating the categorization of either "<u>Pelagian</u>" or "Semi-Pelagian." The latter holds that the first steps are originated by the human will rather than by the Holy Spirit) This doctrine is similar to the Calvinist doctrine of <u>total depravity</u>, with some important <u>differences</u>.

4) **Grace is not irresistible**

(Thus faith is itself a principle or capacity in autonomous natural man standing ultimately independent of God's action of grace) The Reformed Tradition, by contrast, teaches that God can make His grace efficacious

5) **Possibility of falling away from grace**

This is the supposition that our sin as believers can result in God's judicial displeasure. Many Armenians teach that our judicial standing before God must be maintained by holy living. Justification, in other words can be gained and lost. The **Reformed Tradition**, by contrast, maintains the biblical teaching that our judicial standing before God is through Christ's blood, which alone is sufficient to maintain our justification. Holy living and perseverance springs from our new nature received in regeneration which now delights in God's law, and will not fall away.

These Five Points of the Remonstrance of 1610 are virtually identical (prima facie) with Catholic Molinism[37]

According to this information, First, 'election' is conditional instead of unconditional, being based upon man's response by faith. Second, Christ's atonement is viewed as universal, as opposed to particular or limited. Third, God's Grace is not

---

[37] Arminian Five Points of the Remonstrance of 1610 at: http://www.monergism.com/thethreshold/articles/onsite/essential_differences.html

The K.I.S.S. Principle

irresistible as it is according to Calvinism. And lastly, the Armenian view of salvation is that in order for man to keep his salvation, he must maintain holy living. Therefore, even though salvation is obtainable by anyone, it can also be lost.

<u>Denominations</u>
Salvation according to the Lutheran Church

Lutheranism is the name or title that refers to the doctrine and practices of the Lutheran Church. The name "Lutheran" was not a name chosen by those of that particular belief, but was the name applied by the enemies of Martin Luther in the early 1520's. Martin Luther preferred the term "Evangelical". The 16th century reformer was disturbed by the immorality and corruption in the Roman Catholic Church. Yet, he focused or concentrated instead on reforming that which he considered to be corrupt teaching. He proclaimed the message of divine promise and denounced the human merits by or through which, he feared, many if not most Catholics believed would earn them the favor of God. Luther, on the other hand by reading the Bible, came to the conclusion that '*...people are made right with God sola gratia and sola fide - that is, only by the divine initiative of grace as received through God's gift of faith.*'[38] This ultimately would cause him to be excommunicated from the Roman Catholic Church by the Pope.

---

[38] General Information at: http://mb-soft.com/believe/text/lutheran.htm

Rev. Clayton Hampton

Salvation, according to Lutheran teaching, does not depend on worthiness or merit but is a gift of God's sovereign grace. All human beings are considered sinners and, because of original sin, are in bondage to the powers of evil and thus unable to contribute to their liberation (see Justification). Lutherans believe that faith, understood as trust in God's steadfast love, is the only appropriate way for human beings to respond to God's saving initiative. Thus, "salvation by faith alone" became the distinctive and controversial slogan of Lutheranism.

Opponents claimed that this position failed to do justice to the Christian responsibility to do good works, but Lutherans have replied that faith must be active in love and that good works follow from faith as a good tree produces good fruit.[39]

The problem with the opponents in the previous statement is that they appear to merge Christian Service with Christian Salvation, requiring both to be a part of the same belief structure that would have a person believe that if the prospective Christian isn't *Serving* the Lord, then they are not *Saved*! Or, if you are Saved, then you *WILL*

---

[39] Salvation by Faith at: http://mb-soft.com/believe/text/lutheran.htm

The K.I.S.S. Principle

Serve the Lord. However, this doesn't make sense, because if this were true, then there would be no need for God to discipline His child(Heb. 12:6, 12), because they would always be in tune with Him, constantly serving Him. As the quote states, "...*good works follow from faith*...". This simply means that Christian Service is an outgrowth of Christian Salvation, but is not a part of Salvation. Salvation is based upon a person's faith in what Christ did on the cross for them, while Service is based upon what a person does for Christ, as they live their life for Christ daily.

Salvation according to Episcopalian Church

Before providing an explanation of Salvation according to Episcopalians, it may be a good idea to provide an explanation of who the Episcopalians are, or that is, where the Episcopalian Church came from. The Church itself came out of the Church of England, having been organized just after the American Revolution, when it was forced to separate from the Church of England.... *The Episcopal Church describes itself as being "Protestant, Yet Catholic".*[40] Due to the efforts of Bishop William White of Pennsylvania(with his assistance in creating the '39 Articles of Religion'), according to Robert Richard, Episcopalians adopted a common view of the process by which believers attain salvation. According to Mr. Richard, Bishop White

---

[40] Episcopal Church at: http://www.ask.com/wiki/ Episcopal_Church_(United_States)

sought to provide organizational and intellectual shape to the demoralized remnants of the Church of England in America after the War of Independence.

> Because "the nature of salvation" was the principal religious issue about which his contemporaries were concerned, White provided a basic theological and ethical framework for Episcopalians, emphasizing that a person could be assured of salvation if s/he lived in a responsible fashion, was baptized, and participated in the church. Although the evangelical and high church parties stressed different aspects of this formula, each side accepted the essential features of the model White presented.[41]

Below, are four of the articles that appear to provide focus on Salvation:

VI. Of the Sufficiency of the Holy Scriptures for Salvation.

Holy Scripture containeth all things necessary to salvation: so that whatsoever is not read therein, nor may be proved thereby, is not to be required of any

---

[41] Nature of Salvation: Theological consensus in the Episcopal Church, 1807-73, The at: http://findarticles.com/p/articles/mi_qa3818/is_199810/ai_n8820414/?tag=content;col1

man, that it should be believed as an article of the Faith, or be thought requisite or necessary to salvation.

XI. Of the Justification of Man.

We are accounted righteous before God, only for the merit of our Lord and Saviour Jesus Christ by Faith, and not for our own works or deservings. Wherefore, that we are justified by Faith only, is a most wholesome Doctrine, and very full of comfort, as more largely is expressed in the Homily of Justification.

XVIII. Of obtaining eternal Salvation only by the Name of Christ.

They also are to be had accursed that presume to say, That every man shall be saved by the Law or Sect which he professeth, so that he be diligent to frame his life according to that Law, and the light of Nature. For Holy Scripture doth set out unto us only the Name of Jesus Christ, whereby men must be saved.

XXVII. Of Baptism.

Baptism is not only a sign of profession, and mark of difference, whereby Christian men are discerned from others that be not christened, but it is also a sign of Regeneration or New-Birth, whereby, as

> by an instrument, they that receive Baptism rightly are grafted into the Church; the promises of the forgiveness of sin, and of our adoption to be the sons of God by the Holy Ghost, are visibly signed and sealed, Faith is confirmed, and Grace increased by virtue of prayer unto God.[42]

Please note that while all four of these articles appear on the surface to clearly point to salvation by grace through faith, that the actual consensus of what the Episcopalian's believe appears to be '*...a person could be assured of salvation if s/he lived in a responsible fashion, was baptized, and participated in the church*', as stated in one of the excerpts above. This statement very definitely infers that salvation is based on and/or is kept by works. It is easy to see here that what they believe and practice is in direct conflict with what they claim to believe in the '*Articles of Religion*'.

In a statement by one Episcopal Church:

> **The Means of Salvation** – The Episcopal Church teaches that salvation is the divine gift of God, and is made available to us through Jesus Christ our Savior, who stands between us and God the Father, mediating on our behalf. While Salvation is a gift, it is also a lifelong process. Baptism is one

---

[42] Articles of Religion at: http://www.anglicansonline.org/basics/thirty-nine_articles.html

The K.I.S.S. Principle

of the important first steps in beginning
the new life in Christ.[43]

This appears to say that salvation is a gift, but
appears to infer that it is a lifelong process of various steps to get to the point where you actually
receive the gift as opposed to the salvation that
God promises, that appears to be obtained the
instant you trust in Christ.

Salvation according to the Baptist Church
American Baptist Association

It is important to note at this point that you should
not confuse this group with the American Baptist
Churches USA, which was known as the Northern
Baptist Convention from 1907 to 1950.

According to the Doctrinal Statement of the
American Baptist Association in the two points
listed below, they acknowledge that:

> 11. We believe that the suffering and
> death of Jesus Christ was substitu-
> tionary for all mankind and is efficacious
> only to those who believe (Isa. 53:6;
> Heb. 2:9; 1 Peter 2:24; 1 Peter 3:18; 2
> Peter 3:9; 1 John 2:2).

---

[43] A Quickstart Guide to the Episcopal Church at: http://www.stjohnsclear-water.org/quickstartinfo.asp

> 14. We believe that the depraved sinner is saved wholly by grace through faith in Jesus Christ, and the requisites to regeneration are repentance toward God and faith in the Lord Jesus Christ (Luke 13:3-5; John 3:16-18; Acts 20:21; Rom. 6:23; Eph. 2:8, 9), and that the Holy Spirit convicts sinners, regenerates, seals, secures, and indwells every believer (John 3:6; John 16:8, 9; Rom. 8:9-11; 1 Cor. 6:19, 20; Eph. 4:30; Titus 3:5).[44]

These points appear to indicate that they believe a person is saved by grace through faith in the substitutionary payment of Christ for all sin on the cross, specifically the individual's sin. However, in their attempt to explain salvation, they make the whole experience much more complex than I believe God ever intended it to be. They refer to God's simple statement, '...*believe on the Lord Jesus Christ and thou shalt be saved...*' And then, they add in as a part of their explanation of salvation, as they dissect this great passage, their definition of repentance that includes the *sorrow for, and ripping away from a life of sin.* While this author does believe that repentance is a very important and, in fact, necessary part of salvation, I do not believe that the American Baptist have properly translated the word, *repentance.* I say that without providing

---

[44] Doctrinal Statement of the American Baptist Association at: http://www.abaptist.org/general.html

The K.I.S.S. Principle

my understanding of the word, because the definition they provide appears to add something else to the act of faith that God requires. Then their effort to define faith (Plan of Salvation Tract, The Plan of Salvation, III. What Does Jesus Say We Must Do To Be Saved?) appears to provide so much information as to cause the reader to state, 'What?' when they finish reading the explanation, displayed below:

> **Faith.** What is it? "But without faith it is impossible to please him: for he that cometh to God must believe that he is, and that he is a rewarder of them that diligently seek him," Heb. 11:6. Since it is impossible to please God without faith, and God certainly will not receive into His eternal presence anything that displeases Him, we must have faith to abide in His presence. "So then faith cometh by hearing, and hearing by the word of God," Rom. 10:17. When the gospel is preached to a sinner and it finds a responsive attitude from the sinner, it produces faith in the heart of the sinner. Faith is also of three elements: (1) Intellectual; by this the sinner is made to know that God is, and that He rewards them that seek Him. (2) Belief, by the gospel, the sinner comes to believe that Christ can and will save him. (3) Trust. When the sinner knows that God will reward him, and that Christ

> will save him, he is led to trust Christ to save him by surrendering himself wholly into His hands. Repentance furnishes his attitude toward the world of sin, while faith furnishes his attitude toward God and Christ, and the two together cause him to surrender passively into the care and keeping of the Holy Spirit: he being thus prepared, the Holy Spirit begets within him the new life; then, he is saved; he is passed from death into life. He has the same kind of life that is in God, his Father, which is eternal life.[45]

According to the aforementioned definition of **Faith**, it is not only an act of acknowledging who god is, but it is a belief in what He does, in that He rewards those that seek Him, that Christ can and will save the sinner, and those who exhibit faith "...*will surrender their lives completely into His hands.*" This appears to say that if the sinner doesn't completely surrender his/her life into His hand, that they didn't have real faith. That being said, the question needs to be asked, is that person saved? What about the person who exhibits the proper criteria regarding the description of Faith they have provided, but a few years down the road, they fall back into a life of sin. Does this action, in fact, cause a change in that person's salvation? In other words, are they still saved? Because, if they are, then this group

---

[45] The Plan of Salvation at: http://www.abaptist.org/general.html

The K.I.S.S. Principle

needs to reevaluate their description on Faith and what it causes in the believer.

Northern Baptists
or
American Baptist Churches USA

In an effort to ensure that proper documentation is provided for this group, I thought it best to allow them to describe their origin:

> As the acknowledgment that American Baptist life and mission transcends any set geographical area, the Northern Baptist Convention was renamed the American Baptist Convention in 1950. In 1972, in the midst of reorganization that in part reemphasized the congregation-centered mission of the denomination, its name was changed again to American Baptist Churches USA.[46]

After an unsuccessful attempt at locating information regarding this group's joint belief in salvation and/or the presentation of this doctrine, I contacted a representative of the American Baptist Churches USA. The reply to my inquiry regarding their position as a whole on salvation was:

---

[46] American Baptist Churches USA, Our History, American Baptist Life and Mission Today at: http://www.abc-usa.org/what_we_believe/our-history/

> "You will have trouble finding many definitive statements on the web site because Baptists describe themselves as "non-creedal" (although there are many pseudo-Baptist groups that try to impose a creed while claiming to embrace the Baptist distinctive of "soul-freedom"). Of course, local congregations and associations have the privilege of publishing any number of confessions of faith."

With reference to this statement, the word "creed" is defined as:

> "any system, doctrine, or formula of religious belief, as of a denomination. "

or

> "an authoritative, formulated statement of the chief articles of Christian belief, as the Apostles' Creed, the Nicene Creed, or the Athanasian Creed."[47]

If I wanted to press the point, I could say that the statement about being "non-creedal", by definition, means that they are "non-doctrinal". But, I know that this is not what is intended here. Instead, this group holds to the fact that they are Baptists and

---

[47] Dictionary Reference, Creed, at: http://dictionary.reference.com/browse/creed

The K.I.S.S. Principle

are bound together, at least in part, by the fact that they, as a group or denomination, do not subscribe to a so-called creed that they all believe in. The representative stated further that:

> "Most American Baptists would say that we are saved by grace alone through faith alone in Christ alone, but like in any organization of over a million people, there is hardly 100% consensus. "

While I agree, whole heartedly with the last statement, "*...saved by grace alone through faith alone in Christ alone...*", the fact that there is no agreement amongst the group concerning this or the basic presentation of this to an unbeliever, leaves much room for varied interpretation by all parties within the group, of the statement as well as variation in presentation and thus the potential for both clear as well as unclear presentations of this great doctrine.

That being said, it may help us to understand their position a little better by viewing the definition of "Evangelism" that has been adopted by this denomination:

> *Evangelism is the joyous witness of the People of God to the redeeming love of God urging all to repent and to be reconciled to God and each other through faith in Jesus Christ who lived, died, and was raised from the dead, so that being*

> *made new and empowered by the Holy Spirit believers are incorporated as disciples into the church for worship, fellowship, nurture and engagement in God's mission of evangelization and liberation within society and creation, signifying the Kingdom which is present and yet to come.*[48]

I find it very interesting that this group defines the act of "Evangelism" very eloquently, but doesn't say anything about how they perform the act of evangelism. The definition of a group or denomination is:

> *"...a group having a distinctive interpretation of a religious faith and usually its own organization"*[49]

That being said, it would seem that this group of churches that appear to be like minded along beliefs concerning Baptists, would be unified, more so, along doctrinal lines as well as being like minded in their presentation of God's greatest message, Salvation, and thus have information they subscribe to and teach regarding leading a person to the Lord, even if that information only pointed to one verse of scripture and what they believe that verse teaches concerning salvation

---

[48] American Baptist Churches USA, Evangelism at: http://www.abc-usa.org/about-us/evangelism/

[49] Dictionary Reference, Denomination, at: http://dictionary.reference.com/browse/denomination?s=t

The K.I.S.S. Principle

and how it is attained. Please do not misunderstand me, because I am NOT saying that this group is an unscriptural organization, NOR am I saying that they are wrong in their presentation of salvation, mainly because they do not state what their doctrinal position is nor what they believe constitutes salvation. And, I could be wrong on their lack of joint or unified doctrinal position, but the lack of a unified doctrinal position and presentation of the gospel, opens the door very wide to varied interpretations of the scriptures, that might not be in accord with what God intended. After all, He warned Israel in the Old Testament about alliances with those who didn't hold to the beliefs, teachings, commands, etc. that He had given them as well as the consequences of those alliances. And, I am sure that He is just as concerned about the associations we maintain as well, so that we keep His message clear, as He intended it to be.

I believe whole heartedly in soul-freedom or that is, the priesthood of the believer. But, I also believe that the only way I would align in fellowship with a group of believers and/or churches is to ensure that they believe in or hold to doctrinal truths that not only identify them as a Baptist, but more importantly identify them with scriptural teaching on God, Jesus, the Holy Spirit, Heaven, Hell, Salvation, etc. I believe that I am definitely NOT bound by a creed to go to God, but I am bound or linked with other believers, churches, etc. by a unified belief in salvation, and Bible Doctrines as presented or provided in the scriptures themselves.

Rev. Clayton Hampton

Southern Baptists

According to the Doctrinal Statement of the Southern Baptist Convention, the act of salvation appears to be more than just believing on Christ:

IV. Salvation

Salvation involves the redemption of the whole man, and is offered freely to all who accept Jesus Christ as Lord and Saviour, who by His own blood obtained eternal redemption for the believer. In its broadest sense salvation includes regeneration, justification, sanctification, and glorification. There is no salvation apart from personal faith in Jesus Christ as Lord.

A. Regeneration, or the new birth, is a work of God's grace whereby believers become new creatures in Christ Jesus. It is a change of heart wrought by the Holy Spirit through conviction of sin, to which the sinner responds in repentance toward God and faith in the Lord Jesus Christ. Repentance and faith are inseparable experiences of grace.

Repentance is a genuine turning from sin toward God. Faith is the acceptance of Jesus Christ and commitment

The K.I.S.S. Principle

of the entire personality to Him as Lord and Saviour.

B. Justification is God's gracious and full acquittal upon principles of His righteousness of all sinners who repent and believe in Christ. Justification brings the believer unto a relationship of peace and favor with God.

C. Sanctification is the experience, beginning in regeneration, by which the believer is set apart to God's purposes, and is enabled to progress toward moral and spiritual maturity through the presence and power of the Holy Spirit dwelling in him. Growth in grace should continue throughout the regenerate person's life.

D. Glorification is the culmination of salvation and is the final blessed and abiding state of the redeemed.

Genesis 3:15; Exodus 3:14-17; 6:2-8; Matthew 1:21; 4:17; 16:21-26; 27:22-28:6; Luke 1:68-69; 2:28-32; John 1:11-14,29; 3:3-21,36; 5:24; 10:9,28-29; 15:1-16; 17:17; Acts 2:21; 4:12; 15:11; 16:30-31; 17:30-31; 20:32; Romans 1:16-18; 2:4; 3:23-25; 4:3ff.; 5:8-10; 6:1-23; 8:1-18,29-39; 10:9-10,13; 13:11-14; 1 Corinthians 1:18,30;

Rev. Clayton Hampton

6:19-20; 15:10; 2 Corinthians 5:17-20; Galatians 2:20; 3:13; 5:22-25; 6:15; Ephesians 1:7; 2:8-22; 4:11-16; Philippians 2:12-13; Colossians 1:9-22; 3:1ff.; 1 Thessalonians 5:23-24; 2 Timothy 1:12; Titus 2:11-14; Hebrews 2:1-3; 5:8-9; 9:24-28; 11:1-12:8,14; James 2:14-26; 1 Peter 1:2-23; 1 John 1:6-2:11; Revelation 3:20; 21:1-22:5. [50]

The aforementioned excerpt from their Statement of Faith advises in no uncertain terms that not only does Salvation require the act of Repentance and Faith, but that the definition of Repentance is '*...a genuine turning from sin toward God...*', and that Faith is not only '*...the acceptance of Jesus Christ*', but also a '*...commitment of the entire personality to Him as Lord and Saviour.*' This is commonly understood or known as LORDSHIP SALVATION. What that terminology means is that a person(sinner) must make Christ Lord of their life in order to be saved. Or, that is, if Christ isn't Lord of your life, then you are not saved. They appear to interchange terminology such as 'accept the gift' and 'commitment', inferring that the two terms mean the same thing, as:

Are you ready to **accept the gift** of eternal life that Jesus is offering you

---

[50] Doctrinal Statement of the Southern Baptist Convention, Salvation at: http://www.sbc.net/bfm/bfm2000.asp#iv

The K.I.S.S. Principle

right now? Let's review what this **commitment** involves:

I acknowledge I am a sinner in need of a Savior - this is to repent or turn *away* from sin

> I believe in my heart that God raised Jesus from the dead - this is to trust that Jesus paid the full penalty for my sins

> I confess Jesus as my Lord and my God - **this is to surrender control of my life to Jesus**

> I receive Jesus as my Savior forever - this is to accept that God has done *for* me and *in* me what He promised

> If it is your sincere desire to receive Jesus into your heart as your personal Lord and Savior, then talk to God from your heart:

Here's a Suggested Prayer:

"Lord Jesus, I know that I am a sinner and I do not deserve eternal life. But, I believe You died and rose from the grave to make me a new creation and to prepare me to dwell in your presence

> forever. Jesus, come into my life, **take control of my life**, forgive my sins and save me. I am now placing my trust in You alone for my salvation and I accept your free gift of eternal life." [51]

It is unfortunate that they choose to believe and explain these terms this way, because a free gift, as I understand it, doesn't require anything in return. However, according to their definition, if you do not make a commitment to Christ, then you don't or can't have the gift. Does this also mean that if you become a Christian according to their guidelines and then decide at some point afterwards not to allow Jesus to control your life that you then lose your salvation? It just doesn't make sense.

Then to complicate this further, salvation terminology, such as "*Ask Jesus into your heart*" is used to indicate to the person desiring salvation that they are to pray to Jesus to come into their heart and save them. But, what does this terminology or statement mean? While I do not agree completely with the information brought to light in the SBC Voices article, *Why Adults & Children Should NOT "Ask Jesus Into Their Hearts"*[52], it does bring to light the importance of staying with what scripture says, instead of using terminology

---

[51] How to Become a Christian at: http://www.sbc.net/knowjesus/theplan.asp

[52] **Why Adults & Children Should NOT "Ask Jesus Into Their Hearts"** at: http://sbcvoices.com/why-adults-children-should-not-ask-jesus-into-their-hearts/

The K.I.S.S. Principle

that people do not understand. Do I believe that people get *saved* using this terminology? Yes, I believe they do. But, I believe that the individual is getting *saved* NOT because of the terminology, but IN SPITE of the terminology. This terminology is not used just by Southern Baptists, but by many denominations. While those that oppose the use of this terminology will state that it is not in scripture, the proponents of its use try to vindicate their belief in their use of this terminology by saying that this is what Romans 10:9, 10 means:

> [9] That if thou shalt confess with thy mouth the Lord Jesus, and shalt believe in thine heart that God hath raised him from the dead, thou shalt be saved.

> [10] For with the heart man believeth unto righteousness; and with the mouth confession is made unto salvation.

To any student of Biblical Hermeneutics(the science of interpreting the scriptures), this proves to be in error, because what the proponents have done is applied the verses to the terminology, instead of using the actual translation. The Hermeneutical Principal referred to or used here is the *Application Principle*, which simply states:

> The Application Principle is defined as "that principle by which an application of

truth may be made only *after* the correct interpretation has been learned."[53]

Apparently, the proponents of the usage of this terminology, using the aforementioned passage in Romans as scriptural proof are either not aware of Biblical Hermeneutics or chose not to use it in their interpretation/application of the passage in Romans.

As near as this writer can tell, the word/s *believe* or *believeth* are used at least once in each verse, referencing the faith that the individual is to have. But, nowhere in either verse is the individual commanded, requested, etc. to pray or ask the Lord for anything. It simply appears to focus on faith!

Independent Baptists

According to Independent Baptists, Salvation is by Grace through Faith in the finished work of Christ on the cross as the payment for sin:

VI. Salvation

Salvation from our sinful nature and its accompanying punishment can come only through the blood of the Lord Jesus Christ that He shed on the cross for all of mankind. Salvation is by grace

---

[53] The Application Principle, p. 42, Mastering the **Bible**: A Text on **Biblical Hermeneutics** ... Dr. **Mark** G. **Cambron**

The K.I.S.S. Principle

through faith alone. Only by trusting the finished work of Christ and His resurrection from the dead can one be saved from the penalty of sin. All those who by faith have accepted Christ are eternally saved. Everlasting life has become their present possession that they cannot lose.[54]

By virtue of the definition of the word Independent, it is understood that Independent Baptist Churches are, in fact, autonomous, self-governing bodies and do not necessarily themselves or as part of a group of churches fall under or pledge allegiance to any other governing group or authority. The above excerpt comes from a website for '*Whom Shall I Send?*'(SendUs.org), who advertises their site as, 'A Voice for Independent Baptist Missionaries'.

Independent-Baptists.org, a website supporting and/or providing information on Doctrinal Beliefs, etc. of Independent Baptists provides the following concerning their belief of how a person can know they are saved:

In the Bible God gives us the plan of how to be born again which means

to be saved. His plan is simple! You can be **saved** today. How?

---

[54] Statement of Faith at: http://www.sendus.org/statementoffaith.php

First, my friend, you must realize **you are a sinner. "For all have**

sinned, and come short of the glory of God" (Romans 3:23).

Because you are a sinner, **you are condemned to death.** "For the

wages [payment] of sin is death" (Romans 6:23). **This includes eternal**

separation from God in Hell.

"...it is appointed unto men once to die, but after this the judgment" (Hebrews 9:27).

But God loved you so much **He gave His only begotten Son, Jesus, to bear your sin and die in your place.**

"...He hath made Him [Jesus, Who knew no sin] **to**

be sin for us... that we might be made the righteousness of God in Him" (2 Corinthians 5:21).

Jesus had to shed His blood and die. "For **the life** of the

The K.I.S.S. Principle

flesh is **in the blood"** (Lev. 17:11). "...
without shedding of blood

is no remission [pardon]" (Hebrews 9:22).

"...God commendeth His love toward us,
in that, while we were yet sinners,

Christ died for us" (Romans 5:8).

Although we cannot understand how,
God said **my sins and your sins** were
laid upon Jesus and

He died in our place. He became **our
substitute.** It is true. God cannot lie.

My friend, "God...commandeth all men
everywhere to **repent"** (Acts 17:30).

This repentance is a change of mind
that agrees with God that one is a sinner,
and also agrees with what Jesus did for
us on the Cross.

In Acts 16:30-31, the Philippian jailer
asked Paul and Silas: "...'Sirs, what
must **I do to be saved?'** And they said,
**'Believe on the Lord Jesus Christ,
and thou shalt be saved....'"**

Simply believe on Him as **the one who
bore your sin, died in your place,** was

buried, and whom God resurrected. **His resurrection powerfully assures** that the believer can claim everlasting life when Jesus is received as Savior.[55]

Please note that this information indicates that the sinner must repent, which according them is, '*...a change of mind*'. This form of repentance appears to be correct in the view of this writer, because a person does, in fact, change their mind about sin, about the fact that they are a sinner in need of a savior, that Christ is the way of salvation, etc., when they place their faith in Christ as Savior.

Free Will Baptists

The Free Will Baptists state in their Articles of Faith that Salvation is Free:

> **Salvation Free** - God desires the salvation of all, the Gospel invites all, the Holy Spirit strives with all, and whosoever will may come and take of the water of life freely.[56]

Yet, in many of their churches they reveal that our part in the salvation process is not only to believe, but to turn from our sin(their definition for Repent):

---

[55] God's Simple Plan of Salvation at: http://independent-baptists.org/article11.html?&MMN_position=36:36

[56] Articles of Faith – Salvation Free at: http://www.havenfwbchurch.org/fwbinfo.htm

The K.I.S.S. Principle

Now this is *your* part!

1. Believe
Acts 16:31-"Believe on the Lord Jesus Christ, and thou shalt be saved."

2. Repent (Turn from your sins)
Luke 13:3- "Except ye repent, ye shall all likewise perish."

3. Confess your sin to Jesus
I Timothy 2:5- "For there is one God, and one mediator between God and men, the man Christ Jesus."

4. Confess Jesus before other people
Romans 10:11- "For the scripture saith, Whosoever believeth on him shall not be ashamed."

Pray this Prayer:

"Dear Jesus, I know that I am a sinner and I understand that because of this, I only deserve to go to a place called Hell. The best I know how, I turn from my sin and trust you to save me. Thank you for dying on the cross so I could be saved. Thank you for raising yourself from the dead so I can know what it means to be victorious over the sin that is in my life.

Help me as I begin my new life in You!
In Jesus name, Amen!"[57]

While this author does believe that repentance is a part of the salvation experience, I do not believe that the terminology used, 'turning from sin' is the correct definition of the word. Why? Because, 'turning from sin' would be an act performed by man and that would change the salvation experience from a gift into an exchange. Or, in accord with their terminology, you can't be saved unless you 'turn from sin'.

Salvation according to the Methodist Church

As in the case of the Episcopal Church and it's beliefs, it may be a good idea to reveal a part of the history and/or beginnings of the Methodist Church, before sharing their beliefs and/or teaching on salvation. The website at about.com provides the following:

> The Methodist branch of Protestant religion traces its roots back to 1739 where it developed in England as a result of the teachings of John Wesley. While studying at Oxford, Wesley, his brother Charles, and several other students formed a group devoted to study, prayer and helping the underprivileged. They

---

[57] Landmark Free Will Baptist Church – Plan of Salvation at: http://www.lfwbc.org/salvation

The K.I.S.S. Principle

were labeled "Methodist" by their fellow students because of the way they used "rule" and "method" to go about their religious affairs.

The beginning of Methodism as a popular movement began in 1738, when both of the Wesley brothers, influenced by contact with the Moravians, undertook evangelistic preaching with an emphasis on conversion and holiness. Though both Wesley brothers were ordained ministers of the Church of England, they were barred from speaking in most of its pulpits because of their evangelistic methods. They preached in homes, farm houses, barns, open fields, and wherever they found an audience.

Wesley did not set out to create a new church, but instead began several small faith-restoration groups within the Anglican church called the "United Societies." Soon however, Methodism spread and eventually became its own separate religion when the first conference was held in 1744.

George Whitefield (1714-1770) was a minister in the Church of England and also one of the leaders of the Methodist movement. Some believe that he more than John Wesley is the founder of Methodism. He is famous for his part in the Great Awakening movement in America. As a follower of <u>John Calvin</u>, Whitefield parted ways with Wesley over the doctrine of predestination.

Several divisions and schisms occurred throughout Methodism's American history. In 1939, the three branches of American Methodism (the Methodist Protestant Church, the Methodist Episcopal Church, and the Methodist Episcopal Church, South) came to an agreement to reunite under the name "The Methodist Church." This 7.7 million member church prospered on its own for the next twenty-nine years, as did the newly reunited Evangelical United Brethren Church. In 1968, bishops of the two churches took the necessary steps to combine their churches into what has become the second largest Protestant denomination in America, The United Methodist Church.[58]

As mentioned in the provided information above, the United Methodist Church is an outgrowth of the Anglican Church(or Church of England) due, in part, to the evangelical efforts of John and Charles

---

[58] A Brief History of the Methodist Denomination at: <u>http://christianity.about.com/od/methodistdenomination/a/methodishistory.htm</u>

The K.I.S.S. Principle

Wesley, who were ordained ministers of the Church of England. They did not set out to create a new church, but appear to have desired to reform the Church from within, starting several small groups called the "United Societies." It was left up to the American Revolution to actually cause the creation of what we now call the Methodist Church.

Due to John Wesley's teachings, Methodist appear to believe that:

> People can only be saved through faith in Jesus Christ, not by any other acts of <u>redemption</u> such as good deeds.[59]

This would appear to put their belief in line with the Bible passage:

> "For by grace are ye saved through faith: and that not of yourselves: it is the gift of God: Not of works, lest any man should boast."

> ~ Ephesians 2:8, 9

But while Wesley appeared to believe this, he went on to infer in his message "The Scripture Way of Salvation" that other issues, such as repentance, may also have a part in the process:

---

[59] Methodist Doctrine at: http://christianity.about.com/od/devotionals/a/Methodist.htm

Rev. Clayton Hampton

"But does not God command us to repent also? Yea, and to 'bring forth fruits meet for repentance'--to cease, for instance, from doing evil, and learn to do well? And is not both the one and the other of the utmost necessity, insomuch that if we willingly neglect either, we cannot reasonably expect to be justified at all? But if this be so, how can it be said that faith is the only condition of justification?" God does undoubtedly command us both to repent, and to bring forth fruits meet for repentance; which if we willingly neglect, we cannot reasonably expect to be justified at all: therefore both repentance, and fruits meet for repentance, are, in some sense, necessary to justification. But they are not necessary in the *same sense* with faith, nor in the *same degree*. Not in the *same degree*; for those fruits are only necessary *conditionally*; if there be time and opportunity for them. Otherwise a man may be justified without them, as was the *thief* upon the cross (if we may call him so; for a late writer has discovered that he was no thief, but a very honest and respectable person!) but he cannot be justified without faith; this is impossible. Likewise, let a man have ever so much repentance, or ever so many of the fruits meet for repentance, yet all this does not at all avail; he is not

The K.I.S.S. Principle

> justified till he believes. But the moment he believes, with or without those fruits, yea, with more or less repentance, he is justified. --Not in the *same sense*; for repentance and its fruits are only *remotely* necessary; necessary in order to faith; whereas faith is *immediately* necessary to justification. It remains, that faith is the only condition, which is *immediately* and *proximately* necessary to justification. [60]

While I agree that repentance has a role in the salvation experience, I do not agree with the definition of repentance inferred and/or the '...works meet for repentance' mentioned here. First of all, the Greek word for repent, in the referenced verse(Acts 26:20), is μετανοέω or *metanoeō*, and it means 'a change of mind' not a turning from or sorrow for sin. To help explain this, we will take a quick look at the most famous or well known passage in scripture, John chapter 3. If repentance is a necessary part of salvation, why didn't the Lord, in John 3, tell Nicodemus to repent? Why? Because, the word means 'a change of mind'. What did Nicodemus have to do to believe in, or that is have faith in Jesus as his Messiah? He had to 'change his mind'. Did he change his mind? Yes he did, and therefore by definition, *repented*! As for the '...works meet for repentance', Nicodemus'

---

[60] The Scripture Way of Salvation Point III at: http://new.gbgm-umc.org/umhistory/wesley/sermons/43/

Rev. Clayton Hampton

proved or provided this in at least two places. In the first place, he came to him under the cover of night and provides a semi-voluntary confession of Christ to the Pharisees in defense of Jesus in John 7:50-53. Then, in John 19:38-42, he confirms his belief in Christ as he brings the spices for the body of the Lord in preparation for His burial. Those spices, by virtue of their size or amount had to be purchased and therefore someone would have had to know about it. These, in my mind, were Nicodemus' '...works meet for repentance'. His actions showed that he *believed* in Christ.

I went through this brief discussion on Nicodemus to assist you with a better understanding of what Paul is talking about in Acts 26. For, repentance as it is required for salvation is, in fact, 'a change of mind'. It is a change of mind from believing in whatever you believed before or not believing in Christ as the only way to Heaven to believing in Him as the only way to Heaven and trusting in His death payment on the cross for sin as your payment for sin. In Acts 26:20, two things are being stated; repentance and works meet for repentance. One, repentance, that is a very vital part of salvation. And the other, '...works meet for repentance', that deals more specifically with the evidence or testimony of salvation. They may occur at the same time, but they may occur on separate occasions. If Mr. Wesley is referring to '...works meet for repentance' as good works, meaning not sinning or giving to the church or doing anything as a good work to exemplify his life in Christ, etc.,

The K.I.S.S. Principle

then his belief is in obvious conflict with the statement that salvation is '...not of works' in Ephesians 2:8, 9, unless '...works meet for repentance' is not necessary for salvation. According to his evaluation of the issue, he appears to be very vague or unclear on the matter himself. According to his explanation,

> ...the moment he believes, with or without those fruits, yea, with more or less repentance, he is justified. – Not in the *same sense*; for repentance and its fruits are only *remotely* necessary; necessary in order to faith; whereas faith is *immediately* necessary to justification. It remains, that faith is the only condition, which is *immediately* and *proximately* necessary to justification.

referenced in the statement above, the fruits of repentance are only remotely necessary. It is no wonder that the United Methodist Church, as this writer was advised, does not have a uniform Plan of Salvation. Yet, at least one of their churches has provided the following as their belief concerning this Plan:

GOD'S PLAN OF SALVATION

The bottom line is this: we need saving and we can't save ourselves. Good works can't possibly make up for the damage that sin has done to our relationship with God. Only He can save us. Salvation is a gift from God, poured out freely from His grace. It is available to everyone who accepts Jesus as their Lord and Savior. The Bible tells us that there is only one way to Heaven. Jesus said, "I am the way and the truth and the life. No one comes to the Father except through me." (John 14:6) We must have a relationship with Christ. The fact that you're reading this now may be an indication that you are seeking something that is missing in your life. You may just not know how or where to find it. You've come to the right place. All you need to do is to trust Jesus today. The recipe is simple:

1. Admit that you are a sinner. Don't worry, though, you've got a lot of company. We've all sinned and fallen short of God's glory (Romans 3:23). God has made for us a way out—a way to be dead to sin—and the first step is admitting you've got the problem.

2. Be willing to repent of your sin. Repentance doesn't just mean saying you're sorry. It means turning from sin and turning your life God-ward. That doesn't mean you won't ever sin again. It simply means that you will make every effort to live for God, and that

The K.I.S.S. Principle

you will accept God's help in making that happen.

3. Believe that Jesus Christ died for you, that He was buried, and that He rose from the dead. The wages of sin is death. (Romans 6:23) It's the payment we've earned. But the gift of God is eternal life in Jesus Christ. He bore our punishment so that we could stand blameless in front of God. Hallelujah, what a Savior!

4. Through prayer, invite Jesus to be the Lord and Savior of your life. It doesn't have to be fancy or wordy—heartfelt and straightforward will do. Perhaps something like this: Dear God, I realize that I am a sinner who needs forgiveness. I believe that Jesus Christ died for my sin. I want to turn from sin. Jesus, come into my heart and be Lord of my life. Amen.

If you've prayed a prayer like that, welcome to the family of God! Eternal life starts today. There are a few other things that would be good for you to do right now. First, talk to God every day. He loves to hear from us and draws near to us through prayer. Second, find a Bible-based church where Jesus is Lord so that you can worship, fellowship,

Rev. Clayton Hampton

> and serve with your brothers and sisters. Third, read your Bible. This is truly life's instruction book. Lastly, tell others about Christ. Never be ashamed to speak the name of Jesus. It may mean the difference between life and death.[61]

While this may appear to be a valid plan, it has it's flaws, because only two of the points lend credence to salvation '...by grace through faith'. Point 2 infers that the person must be willing to live a godly life in a turning from sin, which is works. And Point 4, infers that the individual is saved by prayer to god sharing that the person is committing to turning from sin and making Jesus the Lord of their life. That too, is works! The work efforts in these two points change salvation from a gift, as mentioned in Eph. 2:8, 9, to an exchange. Or in other words, the individual commits or promises to turn from and and make Jesus Lord of their life and as a result, God saves them. According to Romans 6:23 there is only ONE payment for sin and that payment is DEATH. not being good, turning from sin, making Jesus Lord, etc. The fact is that Jesus fulfilled the requirement for the sin payment on the cross. So, in order for someone to obtain salvation, all they need do is '...believe on the Lord Jesus Christ'(Acts 16:31) and they will be saved. Or that is, they need to trust in His payment as their payment for their sin and in turn, God GIVES

---

[61] God's Plan of Salvation at: http://firstunitedjoplin.com/#/belong/gods-plan-of-salvation

The K.I.S.S. Principle

them eternal life(salvation). Does God want us to do good works? Yes. Does God want us to live our lives in a manner to try not to sin? Yes. Does God want us to submit to the Lord Jesus and His leadership and guidance over us? Yes. But, He doesn't want us to do those things to BE saved. He wants us to do those things, because we ARE saved(Eph. 2:10).

Salvation according to the Presbyterian Church

In discussing the subject at hand, I should probably provide some insight regarding the Presbyterian Church in general. According to an article by Rev. G. Aiken Taylor, Ph.D. on 'What Presbyterians Believe' from the PCA(Presbyterian Church of America) Historical Center,

> 'It is frequently pointed out that the word "Presbyterian" refers to the Eldership and that Presbyterianism, as such, is a form of church government. Presbyterianism is not only a form of government in the Church, but is also a well-defined system of beliefs or of doctrine.'

So as to ensure the solidarity of Presbyterian officers and/or ministers regarding their beliefs, Rev. Taylor goes on to state:

Rev. Clayton Hampton

Presbyterians share with other evangelical churches many basic beliefs. Presbyterians also recognize that earnest Christians may follow other interpretations of the Bible in non-essential matters. But Presbyterians believe that in the Reformed system (another word for Calvinism) the teachings of the Bible are most fully and most accurately set forth. Every Presbyterian officer and minister takes a vow that he believes the Reformed faith to be that system of doctrine which the Bible teaches. Every Presbyterian officer and minister in the Presbyterian Church, moreover, also vows that he will take steps to remove himself from his position should he ever find that his beliefs have taken another direction.[62]

If this is, in fact, true, then apparently they all hold to the same beliefs with regard to Salvation. And according to the statement above, if they change in measure from those beliefs, then the officer/minister must '*...remove himself from his position.*' As for their specific belief regarding salvation:

We believe that all are sinners and totally unable to save themselves from God's displeasure, except by His mercy.

---

[62] What Presbyterians Believe at: http://www.pcahistory.org/documents/believe.html

The K.I.S.S. Principle

> We believe that salvation is by God alone as He sovereignly chooses those He will save. We believe His choice is based on His grace, not on any human individual merit, or foreseen faith.
>
> We believe that Jesus Christ is the eternal Son of God, who through His perfect life and sacrificial death atoned for the sins of all who will trust in Him, alone, for salvation.[63]

On the surface, these statements appear to be right on target with salvation as a free gift from God. However, when examining the second statement you will notice the portion, '*...by God alone as he sovereignly chooses those He will save.*' This portion of the statement on Salvation comes from the Calvinistic teaching on Predestination that teaches that God chooses some to be saved, which also would have to mean that He also chooses some to be lost! To be a whole hearted believer in this, which is John Calvin's second point(Unconditional Election) of his Five Point doctrine or explanation of the Salvation of man, you'd have to answer the question of the place that *free will* has in the salvation experience. I say that, because if man, according to this teaching, is unconditionally elected to be saved, then how can he have the right or opportunity to have any

---

[63] Presbyterian Church in America - What We Believe at: http://www.pcanet.org/general/beliefs.htm

choice in the matter at all? This teaching takes away man's *free will* to choose Christ and places everything on God, who has made the selection of the man and not man the selection of Christ. Lest you be confused on this matter of Predestination and think that this writer doesn't believe in it, let me assure you that I am a whole hearted believer in the *Biblical* teaching on Predestination. I just believe that Calvin's understanding and teaching on the subject isn't what, I believe, is taught in the scriptures. For a brief evaluation of this, read the book of Ephesians. Note all of the instances where 'in Christ', 'in Him', 'in whom', 'in Christ Jesus', etc. are used. All of these statements and or phrases are pointing to the believer being *in Christ*, which is the focal point of the book. This is very important to the understanding of proper scriptural *Predestination*. One of the main passages, if not the main passage, that is used to teach the doctrine of Predestination is:

Ephesians Chapter 1

[3] Blessed [be] the God and Father of our Lord Jesus Christ, who hath blessed us with all spiritual blessings in heavenly places in Christ:

[4] According as he hath chosen us in him before the foundation of the world, that we should be holy and without blame before him in love:

The K.I.S.S. Principle

5 Having predestinated us unto the adoption of children by Jesus Christ to himself, according to the good pleasure of his will,

6 To the praise of the glory of his grace, wherein he hath made us accepted in the beloved.

Many will use this passage to prove that God predestines some to be saved, referring to verse four where the Apostle Paul states, '...*he hath chosen us in him before the foundation of the world...*' However, a proper evaluation of this reveals that what he didn't say was, '...*he hath chosen us **to be** in him before the foundation of the world...*', which is what they are inferring. If the Apostle Paul had said that, then it would have eliminated the *free will* of all to choose Christ. But, since he didn't say that, then how can predestination be Biblical or that is a true or valid doctrine of scripture? I mean how can God, on one hand, say that He chooses us and on another say that we have the free will to choose Him? It really isn't too difficult to understand, when you keep in mind the focal point or phrase of Ephesians, 'in Christ'. You see, God didn't choose us to be in Christ, but He did choose all of those in Christ to go to Heaven. Our place in the equation is that we have the free will to choose whether or not we want to be in Christ. It's some what like an illustration that I have used many times regarding a flight from Atlanta to Boston that I took several years ago. The airline

Rev. Clayton Hampton

had predetermined that they were going to operate a flight that was destined to go from Atlanta to Boston. That was their choice. My choice was whether or not I wanted to be on the flight.

Salvation according to the churches of Christ

According to a statement from the Churches of Christ website: http://church-of-christ.org/, they(the churches of Christ) '...*are undenominational and have no central headquarters or president. The head of the church is none other than Jesus Christ himself (Ephesians 1:22-23). Each congregation of the churches of Christ is autonomous, and it is the Word of God that unites us into One Faith (Ephesians 4:3-6). We follow the teachings of Jesus Christ and his holy Apostles, and not the teachings of man. We are Christians only!* ' They also affirm that they '...*are not affiliated in any manner with the denominational church known as "The United Church of Christ".*' The inception of the churches of Christ would more properly be viewed as the Restoration Movement, where groups withdrawing from the Methodist Episcopal Church(1793), led by James O'Kelly, Baptists in New England(1802), led by Abner Jones and Elias Smith, Presbyterians in Kentucky(1804), led by Barton w. Stone and several other Presbyterian preachers along with Thomas Campbell and his son Alexander Campbell(1809) of what is now West Virginia, decided to wear only the name Christian and declared that they would take the Bible as the "only sure guide to heaven." Members

The K.I.S.S. Principle

of the church of Christ do not conceive of themselves as a new church started near the beginning of the 19th century. Rather, the whole movement is designed to reproduce in contemporary times the church originally established on Pentecost, A.D. 30. The strength of the appeal lies in the restoration of Christ's original church.[64]

While the beliefs and efforts of a few to restore the original New Testament church is commendable, their beliefs and or teaching on the Plan of Salvation appears not to be in line with what God's Word teaches on the subject, as described by them below:

How does one become a member of the church of Christ?

In the salvation of man's soul there are 2 necessary parts: God's part and man's part. God's part is the big part, "For by grace you have been saved through faith, and that not of yourselves, it is the gift if God; not of works, that no man should glory" (Ephesians 2:8-9). The love which God felt for man led him to send Christ into the world to redeem man. The life and teaching of Jesus, the sacrifice on the cross, and

---

[64] The Historical background of the Restoration Movement at: http://church-of-christ.org/who.html#restore

the proclaiming of the gospel to men constitute God's part in salvation.

Though God's part is the big part, man's part is also necessary if man is to reach heaven. Man must comply with the conditions of pardon which the Lord has announced. Man's part can clearly set forth in the following steps:

Hear the Gospel. "How shall they call on him whom they have not believed? and how shall they believe him whom they have not heard? and how shall they hear without a preacher?" (Romans 10:14).

Believe. "And without faith it is impossible to be well pleasing unto him; for he that cometh to God must believe that he is, and that he is a rewarder of them that seek after him" (Hebrews 11:6).

Repent of past sins. "The times of ignorance therefore God overlooked; but now he commandeth men that they should all everywhere repent" (Acts 17:30).

Confess Jesus as Lord. "Behold here is water; What doth hinder me to be baptized ? And Philip said, if thou believeth with all thy heart thou mayest. And he

The K.I.S.S. Principle

answered and said, I believe that Jesus Christ is the Son of God" (Acts 8:36-37).

Be baptized for the remission of sins. "And Peter said unto them, Repent ye, and be baptized everyone of you in the name of Jesus Christ unto the remission of your sins and ye shall receive the gift of the Holy Spirit" (Acts 2:38).

Live a Christian life. "Ye are an elect race, a royal priesthood, a holy nation, a people for God's own possession, that ye may show forth the excellencies of him who called you out of darkness into his marvelous light" (1 Peter 2:9).[65]

Just as in the case of most religious entities, there are parts of their beliefs that appear to be true and/ or correct. However, other parts of their statement on salvation appear to require more than the *faith* that the Bible requires for salvation:

Believe: According to Acts 16:31, '*...believe on the Lord Jesus Christ and thou shalt be saved and thy house.*' This appears to be the only requirement, according to the Apostle Paul, for salvation. The word *believe* comes from the Greek word 'πιστεύω'(*pisteuō*), which means 'to think to be true, to be persuaded of'. The word *Lord* comes

---

[65] How does one become a member of the church of Christ? at: http://church-of-christ.org/who.html#restore

from the Greek word κύριος(*kü'-rē-os*), which is a title that directs one's attention more to *who* Jesus Christ is than to *what* He wants them to do. In other words, the individual is instructed to believe that He(Jesus) is the *Lord* or God who not only has the power to save, but has actually made the only payment possible for salvation. When an individual does this, they appear to be accepting the fact that not only is He God, but also the payment that Jesus made on the cross for sin as their own payment for their sin. And Paul says that when they do that, they are saved!

Repent of past sins: There is no question about the fact that the Lord would have us to *repent* as a part of the salvation process. However, it would behoove us to ask, 'what do *they* mean by, *repent of past sins*?' Also, you might ask, 'What about my future sins? What do I do about them?   D o   I need to repent of them as well to remain saved?'

Confess Jesus as Lord: According to the definition provided under this section, above, they appear to equate the title of *Lord* to or with the person of *God*. With this, I would heartily agree, as I have elaborated upon in the information on **Believe**.

Be baptized for the remission of sins: In order to agree with this statement as they intend it, you would have to believe that Jesus' payment for sin on the cross wasn't enough to completely pay for sin. In other words, in order to be saved, not only

The K.I.S.S. Principle

do you have to believe in Christ's payment on the cross, but you also need to be baptized. Now, while this writer believes that the Bible teaches that a believer should be baptized, this is done to give testimony of the believer's salvation experience, not as a requirement for salvation.

Live a Christian life: While this is an obvious valid concern for each and every Christian, the Bible doesn't state that this something that is required for salvation. If so, then you'd also have to say that if a believer stopped living a Christian life they were no longer saved. This would mean that, as mentioned in the previous information on **Be baptized for the remission of sins,** the payment Christ made on the cross was not sufficient to pay for our sins, but that in addition to that payment, we need to live a Christian life to be saved.

Salvation according to the United Church of Christ

To say that it would take a fair amount of space to explain just how the United Church of Christ came into being is an understatement. Suffice it to say that two groups, the Congregational Christian Churches(formed on June 17, 1931) and the Evangelical and Reformed Church(formed June 26, 1934) united on June 25, 1957 to form the United Church of Christ. These denominations sought to unite based more upon that which unites Christians than what divides them. This can and

Rev. Clayton Hampton

does really present problems when what divides them is their belief concerning salvation.

According to most of the information researched on the subject of Salvation or that is, the question, 'What must a person do to be saved?', it was found that the United Church of Christ/Congregationalism beliefs on salvation appear to vary:

> Congregationalists gradually turned away from Calvinist teachings on predestination. UCC congregants hold a range of views on the afterlife, with some believing in universalism, or the idea that ultimately all humans will be reconciled to God.[66]

While I understand that, according to the statement above, not all UCC churches believe in universalism, the fact that some do really presents issues that conflict with what scripture teaches on the subject of salvation and I would think cause a serious division within the UCC. But, apparently it doesn't. Remember that the unification that took place in 1957 was concerned more with what '... unites Christians than what divides them.'

Then, there are those in the UCC like Fed D. Ranches, Minister of Evangelism for Local Church Development and Renewal, Local Church

---

[66] United church of Christ Beliefs at: http://www.patheos.com/Library/United-Church-of-ChristCongregationalism/Beliefs.html

Ministries United Church of Christ who believe teaching that Salvation is free is to teach that it is cheap:

Salvation is free and cheap

The emphasis on "free salvation" has neglected the theology of the cross. The costliness of God's grace is forgotten. It has made "salvation" cheap and easy: "Just believe and you are saved." Yet, salvation cost God, the death of his only Son on the cross to make humankind free. Such freedom, because it is precious, becomes a costly responsibility. A theological perspective that calls for the "wholeness of life" must be the basis of our evangelism or else we shall fall into the same temptation of schisms and divisiveness.[67]

However, while Salvation is free/gift according to Ephesians 2:8, it is not cheap, because it cost God's son his life! According to Mr. Ranches in the statement above, this '...calls for the "wholeness of life" as a basis of our evangelism.' But, what does that really mean? Does it mean that a person must dedicate their whole life to the Lord when they believe that Christ died for their sins? If so, that is making *works* a part of the

---

[67] Evangelism + Development = Mission of the Church at: http://www.ucc. org/evangelism/e-word/4EvangelismPlusDevelopment.pdf

salvation experience, which is in direct opposition to Ephesians 2:9, where it states that salvation is '*...not of works, lest any man should boast.*' I agree with him in saying that salvation is precious. But, I do not agree that salvation not only cost God's son his life, but also the prospective believer the apparent "*wholeness of life*" commitment that he infers that a person needs as well.

Salvation according to the Christian Church (The Disciples of Christ)

It would be good to remember at this point that the *Christian Church(The Disciples of Christ)*, *The churches of Christ* and the *United Church of Christ* appear to be closely linked together theologically, having come from an intermixture of beliefs that permeated the various churches as the various belief systems united. However, they appear to be united with regard to the teachings on Salvation. Put simply, the Christian Church(The Disciples of Christ) hold to the same teachings on salvation as mentioned in the previous section for the churches of Christ, or *Hear, Believe, Repent, Confess, Baptism, and Christian life in the church.*[68]

One thing that I found very interesting was the varied notable or prominent members, ranging from U.S.

---

[68] How does one become a Christian, point 1.5.2 at: http://www.northcantonccc.org/templates/System/details.asp?id=39908&PID=560885

The K.I.S.S. Principle

Presidents to Psychics to Business Personalities to Legendary Coaches, as shown below:

> **Prominent Members:** Edgar Cayce(psychic and healer), James Garfield(20th President of the United States), Lyndon Baines Johnson(36th President of the United States), James Warren "Jim" Jones(founder of the Peoples Temple of Jonestown, Guyana, though disaffiliated with the church before founding the People's Temple), Ronald Reagan(40th President of the United States), Colonel Sanders(founder of Kentucky Fried Chicken), and John Wooden(legendary UCLA basketball coach).[69]

While many of these individuals either are or were very well respected, it also becomes apparent that belief in a theological viewpoint is no respecter of persons. Many of these individuals accomplished great things in their human life and were highly respected. But, that doesn't mean that their theological viewpoint was correct. We need to be careful to judge the individual by what God's Word says and not the other way around.

---

[69] Christian Church (Disciples of Christ) at: http://en.wikipedia.org/wiki/Christian_Church_(Disciples_of_Christ)

Rev. Clayton Hampton

Salvation according to the Pentecostal Church

The term *Pentecostalism* in and of itself is a term that spans across several denominations including a wide range of different theologies and cultures. However, that being said, here we will not be referencing the term, but the Pentecostal Church. According to the United Pentecostal Church, Salvation is by Grace through Faith in Chirst's finished work on the cross, burial and resurrection. Yet, to elaborate with more detail, *saving faith involves the acceptance of the gospel of Jesus Christ as the means of salvation and obedience to that gospel(application or appropriation of that gospel).*

New Testament Salvation

Salvation is by grace through faith and not by human works (Ephesians 2:8-9). The doctrine of grace means that salvation is a free gift from God, which humans cannot merit or earn; in other words, salvation is God's work in us. The atoning death, burial, and resurrection of Jesus Christ have made this gift available.

The doctrine of faith means that we receive God's saving work by trusting in Jesus Christ. Faith is more than mental assent, intellectual acceptance,

The K.I.S.S. Principle

or verbal profession; it includes trust, reliance, appropriation, and application. Faith is alive only through response and action; we cannot separate faith from obedience. (See Matthew 7:21-27; Romans 1:5; 6:17; 10:16; 16:26; II Thessalonians 1:7-10.) Saving faith, then, is (1) acceptance of the gospel of Jesus Christ as the means of salvation and (2) obedience to that gospel (application or appropriation of that gospel).

The gospel of Jesus Christ is His death, burial, and resurrection for our salvation (I Corinthians 15:1-4). On the Day of Pentecost, the birthday of the New Testament church, the apostle Peter preached the first gospel sermon to the crowds who had gathered to observe the Spirit-filled believers as they spoke in tongues and worshiped God. He proclaimed the death, burial, and resurrection of Jesus Christ. Convicted of their sins by his simple yet powerful message, the audience cried out, "Men and brethren, what shall we do?" (Acts 2:37). Peter, with the support of the other apostles, gave a precise, complete, and unequivocal answer: "Repent, and be baptized every one of you in the name of Jesus Christ for the remission of sins, and ye shall receive the gift of the Holy Ghost" (Acts 2:38). As this

Rev. Clayton Hampton

verse shows, we respond to the gospel, obey the gospel, or apply the gospel to our lives by repentance from sin (death to sin), water baptism by immersion in the name of Jesus Christ (burial with Christ), and receiving the Holy Spirit (new life in Christ). (See Romans 6:1-7; 7:6; 8:2, 10.)

This response is the biblical expression of saving faith in Jesus Christ. (See Mark 1:15; 16:16; John 7:37-39; Acts 11:15-17.) This threefold experience, viewed as an integrated whole, brings regeneration, justification, and initial sanctification. (See I Corinthians 6:11; Titus 3:5.) Baptism of water and Spirit is the birth of water and Spirit, the born-again experience of which Jesus spoke in John 3:3-5. The three steps are not human works that earn salvation but divine works of salvation in human lives.

Thus, Acts 2:38 is the comprehensive answer to an inquiry about New Testament conversion, expressing in a nutshell the proper response to the gospel. Not only did Jews from many nations on the Day of Pentecost receive the Acts 2:38 experience, but so did all other converts in the New Testament, including the Samaritans, the apostle

The K.I.S.S. Principle

> Paul, the Gentiles at Caesarea, and the disciples of John at Ephesus.
>
> In each case, believers were baptized with the invocation of the name of Jesus, even some who had previously been baptized another way. (See Acts 2:38; 8:16; 10:48; 19:3-5; 22:16.) The Epistles also allude repeatedly to the Jesus Name formula. (See Romans 6:3-4; I Corinthians 1:13; 6:11; Galatians 3:27; Colossians 2:12.) Moreover, the examples in Acts show that the baptism of the Spirit is for everyone and is accompanied by the initial sign of tongues. (See Acts 2:4; 10:44-47; 19:6.) The experience signified by tongues is the promised outpouring of the Spirit (Acts 2:6-17, 33).[70]

As in most cases when discussing theological viewpoints and/or doctrinal positions, it is important to not only present their statement from scripture, but elaborate on or bring to light the individual components of the referenced belief. They propose that the salvation experience is made up of three parts, a response to/obedience to/application of the gospel by repenting of sin, experiencing water baptism, and receiving of the Holy Spirit(baptism of the Holy Spirit):

---

[70] New Testament Salvation at: http://www.upci.org/component/content/article/83-beliefs/91-our-doctrinal-foundation

> The doctrine of salvation: We enter into the New Testament church through faith in Jesus as Lord and Savior, repentance from sin, water baptism in the name of Jesus Christ, and the baptism of the Holy Spirit with the initial sign of tongues. (See Acts 2:1-4, 36-39; 11:13-17.)[71]

They advise that none of these actions are considered as human works, stating, "*The three steps are not human works that earn salvation but divine works of salvation in human lives.*" However, if this is true, then why are the same actions not given consideration every time that eternal salvation is mentioned thereafter in scripture. In Acts 16 the Apostle Paul and Silas his assistant were in jail in Phillippi. At midnight, in their bonds, they began to pray and sing and there was a great shaking in the jail resulting in the jail doors opening and their bonds loosened. The jailor. who was obviously frightened by the situation, stuck his head into their cell(realizing his consequences, if any should any escape) and said, "*What **must** I do to be saved?*" The Apostle didn't say, repent, be baptized and receive the Holy Spirit. He stated simply and emphatically, "*Believe on the Lord Jesus Christ and thou shalt be saved.*" According to this statement, either one of two things are true. Either the Apostle Paul lied, telling the man that all he

---

[71] The Apostolic Message, The doctrine of Salvation, at: http://www.upci. org/component/content/article/83-beliefs/91-our-doctrinal-foundation

The K.I.S.S. Principle

need to do was…*believe on the Lord Jesus Christ* or the doctrinal position set forth by the United Pentecostal Church regarding salvation is wrong. According to their statement on the doctrine of salvation, shown above, do they also hold that if a person *believes on the Lord Jesus Christ*, but is not water baptized or doesn't speak in tongues that that individual isn't saved? What about the thief on the cross that was speaking directly to the Lord? Did the Lord, himself, lie to him(that couldn't be water baptized and certainly didn't evidence the indwelling Holy Spirit by speaking in tongues) saying,…*this day thou shalt be with me in paradise*?

This writer contends that everyone, from the beginning of time to the end of time are saved in the same way/manner. That is, they are "…*saved by grace through faith*" in the finished work of Christ on the cross as payment for their sins.

Salvation according to the Church of God

The United Church of God, as opposed to using a formulated list of steps to salvation as many do, appear to have chosen to use the vehicle of Scripture to explain their beliefs on Salvation via their focus on or their interpretation of Acts 2:38 :

> Then Peter said unto them, Repent, and be baptized every one of you in the name of Jesus Christ for the remission

of sins, and ye shall receive the gift of
the Holy Ghost.(KJV)

As in many, if not most, cases, they define salvation as the means of rescuing...*someone from the eternal consequences of sin.*[72] They go on to explain that while we are all sinners that our sin debt(death) was paid by Christ on the cross and that to obtain this salvation,...*You must accept Jesus as your personal Savior, recognizing that He died for you.*[73] This appears to be a simple enough task. This is where they begin to focus on Acts 2:38, which was mentioned above, to bring to light their view that repentance plays in the salvation process.

What must we do?

To have Jesus Christ as your Savior
you must acknowledge that you have
sinned, that your sins have placed you
under a sentence of death and that you
need forgiveness through Christ's sacrifice. You must then accept Jesus as
your personal Savior, recognizing that
He died for you.

Regrettably, many people stop right
there and think that's all there is to it.

---

[72] Salvation is God's Plan at: http://www.ucg.org/salvation/

[73] What must we do? at: http://www.ucg.org/salvation/

The K.I.S.S. Principle

They fail to recognize the crucial necessity of *personal repentance*.

In recognition of Christ's sacrifice and with a desire to change our lives to please God, each of us must forsake the sinful ways that brought the death penalty upon us and made Jesus' sacrifice necessary in the first place. We must undergo a life-transforming change of heart and direction, a process the Bible calls repentance.

Peter said, "Repent, and let every one of you be baptized in the name of Jesus Christ for the remission of sins; and you shall receive the gift of the Holy Spirit" (**Acts 2:38**). Remission means release—that is, release from guilt for your sins. When you are baptized, God forgives your past sins and clears your record.

Baptism pictures the washing away of sins and signifies our faith in the sacrifice of Christ as payment for them. After our baptism, Christ's ministers are to place their hands on us and pray for the gift of God's Spirit for us. It is at this point that God gives His Spirit to a repentant, baptized person (see **Acts:8:18** And when Simon saw that through laying on of the apostles' hands the Holy Ghost was given, he offered them money,).

The Bible says that, through the Holy Spirit, God *seals* us, His Spirit serving as a *guarantee* of or *down payment* on our salvation (**2 Corinthians:1:22** Who hath also sealed us, and given the earnest of the Spirit in our hearts.). The reason for this guarantee is to assure us we will receive eternal life. In other words, our sealing with the Holy Spirit is the proof we belong to God and Christ. "Now if anyone does not have the Spirit of Christ, he is not His" (**Romans: 8:9** But ye are not in the flesh, but in the Spirit, if so be that the Spirit of God dwell in you. Now if any man have not the Spirit of Christ, he is none of his.), and "as many as are led by the Spirit of God, these are the sons of God" (verse 14).

After baptism and our receiving of God's Spirit, we are justified—that is, we become righteous in God's sight. God counts none of our past sins against us (**Romans: 3:25** Whom God hath set forth to be a propitiation through faith in his blood, to declare his righteousness for the remission of sins that are past, through the forbearance of God;). If we stumble and sin after baptism, we must ask God's forgiveness and return

The K.I.S.S. Principle

to Him so that our state of forgiveness is not lost by our return to our old sinful way of life (**1 John: 2:1-6** [1]My little children, these things write I unto you, that ye sin not. And if any man sin, we have an advocate with the Father, Jesus Christ the righteous:[2]And he is the propitiation for our sins: and not for our's only, but also for the sins of the whole world.[3]And hereby we do know that we know him, if we keep his commandments.[4]He that saith, I know him, and keepeth not his commandments, is a liar, and the truth is not in him.[5]But whoso keepeth his word, in him verily is the love of God perfected: hereby know we that we are in him.[6]He that saith he abideth in him ought himself also so to walk, even as he walked.). When we are justified, God deals with us as though we had never sinned; the death penalty has no hold on us.

We must endure faithfully to the end of our lives. If a Christian at some time during his life, after committing to serve God, turns away and renounces Jesus and God's way in word or action, he will *lose* his salvation—unless he repents of his error.[74]

---

[74] What must we do? at: http://www.ucg.org/salvation/

Rev. Clayton Hampton

Actually, several issues(repentance, baptism, and eternal security) are brought to bear in the referenced information above. The view therein appears to equate or define repentance with a for-saking of ones sinful ways or that is *a life-trans-forming change of heart and direction.* Also, after baptism(while only a symbol, it appears to be an essential part of the process) Christ's ministers are to lay hands on the individual and pray for God's spirit for the them. At this point, God gives His Spirit to the repentant person. The following state-ments indicate the fact that since the individual now has God's Spirit, they are now seen as being justified or righteous in God's sight. Then they go on to state that the individual must continue along this line OR they will lose their salvation.

Their view of repentance appears to be an act by the individual to stop sinning as opposed to simply changing their mind about the fact that they are a sinner in need of a savior and that to change from that action invokes a loss of salvation. This is nothing more than works and changes the gift of God into an exchange. Instead of simply accepting God's gift, His gift of salvation appears to depend on whether we are willing to stop sinning, etc.

Salvation according to the Church of the Nazarene

The Church of the Nazarene approach to salvation is explained in their dissertation on *How to Know Jesus*, shown below:

The K.I.S.S. Principle

How to Know Jesus

1. Recognize that God loves you and has a plan for your life.

His love includes you.

"For God so loved the world that he gave his one and only Son, that whoever believes in him shall not perish but have eternal life" (John 3:16).

He has new life for you.

"I have come that they may have life, and have it to the full" (John 10:10).

2. Recognize that sin separates you from God and others.

"Sin" is walking our own way in rebellion against God's will. When we walk away from God, we walk away from life.

Everyone has sinned.

"For all have sinned and fall short of the glory of God" (Romans 3:23).

Sin brings death.

"For the wages of sin is death" (Romans 6:23).

Our own efforts cannot save us.

As sinners we futilely try to find life's true meaning in the wrong ways and places.

"For it is by grace you have been saved, through faith-and this not from yourselves, it is the gift of God-not by works, so that no one can boast" (Ephesians 2:8-9).

3. Recognize that Jesus Christ died and rose again for our sins.

Jesus Christ died in our place.

"But God demonstrates his own love for us in this: While we were still sinners, Christ died for us" (Romans 5:8).

He is the way to new life.

"Therefore, if anyone is in Christ, he is a new creation; the old has gone, the new has come!" (2 Corinthians 5:17).

The K.I.S.S. Principle

He gives inner peace.

"We have peace with God through our Lord Jesus Christ" (Romans 5:1).

He gives freedom.

"So if the Son sets you free, you will be free indeed" (John 8:36).

He gives eternal life.

"But the gift of God is eternal life in Christ Jesus our Lord" (Romans 6:23).

4. You must repent and ask God for forgiveness.

Admit and confess your sins to God.

"He who conceals his sins does not prosper, but whoever confesses and renounces them finds mercy" (Proverbs 28:13).

Repentance means:

• To acknowledge your sins.

• To be sorry for your sins.

- To confess your sins.

- To be willing to forsake your sins.

- To have your life changed by Christ.

Forgiveness is promised.

"If we confess our sins, he is faithful and just and will forgive us our sins and purify us from all unrighteousness" (1 John 1:9).

5. Place your trust in Christ and receive Him as your Savior.

Christ is ready.

"Here I am! I stand at the door and knock. If anyone hears my voice and opens the door, I will go in" (Revelation 3:20).

Receive him now.

"Yet to all who received him, to those who believed in his name, he gave the right to become children of God" (John 1:12).

Pray this prayer:

> Lord Jesus, I want to have life. I
> know that I have sinned. I need
> Your forgiveness and pardon. I
> believe that You died and rose
> again for my sins. I now accept
> You as my personal Savior. I will
> forsake my sinful life. I know
> that Your grace and power will
> enable me to live for You. Thank
> You, Jesus, for saving me and
> for giving me a new life. [75]

Please note that as in most discussions on salvation, there are a few points of agreement, such as recognizing that an individual is a sinner, and that fact brings about a debt or sentence for sin which is death. Then, the individual must acknowledge that the payment for their sin was made by Jesus and accept His payment as their payment for sin. The fact that **Repentance** is brought into the process isn't an issue. But, the definition they ascribe to it is. According to the display above, they state that:

Repentance means:

- To acknowledge your sins.

- To be sorry for your sins.

---

[75] How to Know Jesus at: http://nazarene.org/ministries/administration/visitorcenter/knowjesus/display.html

Rev. Clayton Hampton

- To confess your sins.

- To be willing to forsake your sins.

- To have your life changed by Christ.

This writer agrees with the fact that **Repentance** is an essential part of salvation. But, if their definition or meaning of the term is true, then why didn't Jesus tell Nicodemus in John 3 that he needed to either repent or be sorry for his sins or confess his sins and be willing to forsake his sins, etc.? Well, the reason He didn't, is because the word and/or term repent, as opposed to what they propose it to mean, simply means *a change of mind*. And, He didn't tell Nicodemus to repent, because in order for Nicodemus to be saved(or become a Christian) he had to *change his mind* about what he currently believed about himself, that he was a sinner, and his way of resolving the sin question to just believing in Christ(who He was, what He came to do, etc.)

> For the Son of man is come to seek and to save that which was lost.
>
> ~ Luke 19:10(KJV)

I believe that Nicodemus changed his mind, believed on Christ and was saved.

The K.I.S.S. Principle

Christian Organizations
National & Worldwide Interfaith Church Organizations

It should be noted here that the only reason for including the two following entries is due to their apparent claim to be Christian based organizations.

Salvation according to the World Council of Churches

By definition, the World Council of Churches is *a worldwide fellowship of 349 churches seeking unity, a common witness and Christian service*.[76] This is not the proper format for a lengthy discussion on the WCC. So, I'll just state that it is an ecumenical movement that brings together into fellowship different denominations and church fellowships in over 110 countries representing over 560 million Christians.

> "The primary purpose *of the fellowship of churches in the World Council of Churches is to call one another* to visible unity in one faith and in one eucharistic fellowship, expressed in worship and common life in Christ, *through witness and service to the world*, and to

---

[76] World Council of Churches at: http://www.oikoumene.org/

> advance towards that unity in order that
> the world may believe". [77]

Apparently, their belief on salvation is as varied as the number of different denominations and/ or churches that belong to the WCC, as found in *Study V: The Experience of Salvation*.[78] While the study does mention, in part, eternal salvation, it focuses on the various ways salvation is referenced that includes, but is not limited to *eternal life, belonging to the kingdom of God, following Jesus, liberty to captives, setting the oppressed free* and even the linking to *the redemption of the whole created order*, etc.

Salvation according to the National Council of Churches

Like the World Council of Churches, the National Council of Churches is an ecumenical Christian body that contains or embraces a large number of denominations. Among but not limited to these are the American Baptist churches in the USA, the Christian Church(Disciples of Christ), The Episcopal Church, the Evangelical Lutheran Church in America, the National Baptist Convention of America, the Presbyterian Church(U.S.A.), the

---

[77] Self-understanding and vision: Purpose at: http://www.oikoumene.org/en/who-are-we/self-understanding-vision.html

[78] Study V: The Experience of Salvation at: http://www.oikoumene.org/en/resources/documents/wcc-programmes/interreligious-dialogue-and-cooperation/christian-identity-in-pluralistic-societies/study-guide-my-neighbours-faith-and-mine/study-v-the-experience-of-salvation.html

The K.I.S.S. Principle

United Church of Christ, and The United Methodist Church. That being said, it is not difficult to understand that while all of the members believe in Christ, it isn't very well documented if the NCC has a specific doctrinal belief concerning Christ accept:

Statement of Faith

"The National Council of Churches is a community of Christian communions, which, in response to the gospel as revealed in the Scriptures, confess Jesus Christ, the incarnate Word of God, as Savior and Lord.

These communions covenant with one another to manifest ever more fully the unity of the Church.

Relying upon the transforming power of the Holy Spirit, the communions come together as the Council in common mission, serving in all creation to the glory of God."[79]

In the text above, as well as most of the NCC data, the word 'communions' is used as a synonym of the word 'denomination' or 'church'. As I understand it, their goal is to bring into one union all of the various Christian, so called, churches and/

---

[79] About the National Council of Churches, Statement of Faith at: http://www.nationalcouncilofchurches.us/?page=about_us

Rev. Clayton Hampton

or denominations, even though they don't agree on what many would consider important doctrinal positions, etc. like *Salvation*.

However, the *Becker Bible Studies Library of the National Council of Churches* does provide a little more detail with regard to their belief on Salvation. According to this information, they hold to the following:

Salvation

Salvation involves the redemption of the whole man, and is offered freely to all who accept Jesus Christ as Lord and Saviour, who by His own blood obtained eternal redemption for the believer. In its broadest sense salvation includes regeneration, justification, sanctification, and glorification. There is no salvation apart from personal faith in Jesus Christ as Lord.

A. Regeneration, or New Birth, is a work of God's grace whereby believers become new creatures in Christ Jesus at the moment a faithful believer is resurrected out of the Baptismal waters. The Baptism of Jesus Christ brings death to sin, and becomes the grave to which faithful believers in Jesus Christ's own Resurrection, are Born Again as they come up out of the waters. This

The K.I.S.S. Principle

regen-erative process brings a change of heart, forever changed, and a new life able to receive and be guided by the Holy Spirit.

B. Justification is God's gracious and full acquittal upon principles of His righteousness of all sinners who repent and believe in Christ. Justification brings the believer unto a relationship of peace and favor with God.

C. Sanctification is the experience, beginning in regeneration, by which the believer is set apart to God's purposes, and is enabled to progress toward moral and spiritual maturity through the presence and power of the Holy Spirit dwelling in him. Growth in grace should continue through-out the regenerate person's life.

D. Glorification is the culmination of salvation and is the final blessed and abiding state of the redeemed.[80]

Except for a modification of point A., above, this statement by the NCC is an exact restatement of the Doctrinal Statement on the act of Salvation by the Southern Baptist Convention. The Southern

---

[80] Becker bible Studies Authors and Teachers Statement of Faith, Salvation, as: http://www.guidedbiblestudies.com/faith.htm

Rev. Clayton Hampton

Baptist end the first sentence of point A with a period after '...*become new creatures in Christ Jesus*.' The NCC extends the statement to include water baptism as a part of the regenerative process. In other words, they seem to believe that the individual is not regenerated(or born again) until they are '...*resurrected out of the Baptismal waters*.'

While Water Baptism is a vital part of the Christian Life as one of the two ordinances of the Church, according to Scripture we are saved by '...*grace through faith and not of works*'(Eph. 2:8, 9). And, Water Baptism has nothing to do with the act of salvation. All it does do is validate outwardly that which has taken place inwardly.

These additional requirements placed upon the individual make it even more difficult for a person to accept the Lord Jesus as Saviour, indicating that if they are not baptized, then they are not saved or regenerated or born again.

One of the main problems with the NCC is that they freely admit in the Becker Bible Studies on Salvation Fundamentals(<u>Salvation Handout</u>) that '*One of the great divisions among Faithful Christians is caused because they define Salvation differently*.' Yet, they don't appear to think this major doctrinal difference is something to be concerned about when linking together various denominations and/ or beliefs. One point in this document that is very true is, '*If only we could get this definition nailed down, and agree on this one important concept in*

The K.I.S.S. Principle

our Christian faith, then many of the splinters and chasms between our Faithful brothers and sisters could be healed.' The problem is how would they define it. I say that because they have so many varied beliefs as a part of their membership, that I am unaware of, where any two that would be willing to agree on this, without giving up something of doctrinal value to them.

Basically, a more in depth reading of this document reveals that the NCC apparently believes in a works based Salvation as opposed to their initial statement that Salvation is based on faith. Then further into the document they state:

STEPS TO SALVATION

1. Know that you are a sinner, and cannot save yourself.

2. Confess the Lord Jesus Christ as your Saviour.

3. Believe that Jesus Christ's sacrifice was sufficient to atone for your sins.

4. Be confident that Jesus Christ physically rose from the dead.

It may seem like I am nit picking, but the steps listed above appear to be out of order and do not even bring *faith* into the picture. And the NCC wonders why people are confused over this.

Rev. Clayton Hampton

<u>Youth & College</u>
Salvation according to the Fellowship of Christian Athletes

This organization draws many believers from various Christian denominations and therefore it could be said that the way of Salvation within could depend upon who you are talking to at the time. However, FCA does have the New Testament that they print based on the Holman Christian Standard Bible translation. This publication is printed with the intent of reaching out to those involved in sports including pictures scattered throughout its pages of various known sports figures who happen to be Christians. At the end of the publication, is a copy of their apparent belief on Salvation contained within their tract, *'More than Winning, Your Game Plan For Life.'* While the tract provides much more information than just on Salvation, the basic information can be seen in the portion called, *'Replay of God's Plan'* where we find the following:

Replay of God's Plan

REalize God is holy and perfect; we are sinners and cannot save ourselves.

REcognize who Jesus is and what He's done as our substitute.

REceive Jesus Christ by faith as Savior and Lord.

The K.I.S.S. Principle

"But to all who did receive Him, He gave them the right to become children of God,to those who believe in His name..."

John 1:12,13

REspond to Jesus Christ in a life of obedience.

"If anyone wants to come with me, he must deny himself, take up his cross daily, and follow Me." Jesus, Luke 9:23

Does God's plan make sense to you? Are you willing to repent and receive Jesus Christ? If so, express to God your need for him. Consider the "Suggested Prayer of Commitment" on the next page. Remember that God is more concerned with your attitude than with the words you say.

Suggested

Prayer of Commitment

"Lord Jesus, I need you. I realize I'm a sinner and I can't save myself. I need your forgiveness. I believe that you loved me so much that you died on the cross for my sins and rose from the dead. I repent of my sins and put my faith in you as Savior and Lord. Take control of my life and help me to follow you in obedience. I love you Jesus. In Jesus' name, Amen." [81]

It is apparent to me that they use terminology or words that can have different meanings or with meanings that have different points of reference. For instance, the word *commitment*. Is this word or term inferring that the individual is committing their life to Christ, or are they saying that the person is committed to the belief that Christ's payment is sufficient for their sin, etc.? I say that, not to appear nitpicky, but to make a point. Being committed to the belief that Christ's payment is sufficient for their sin and accepting His payment as their payment for their sin is *salvation*. Making a commitment of your life to Christ is *service*. For, salvation is totally '*...by grace through faith...*', plus nothing, minus nothing.

Salvation according to Campus Crusade for Christ

This organization appears to be an independent organization that has many members from various denominations and whose main purpose is '*... helping to fulfill the Great Commission in the power of the Holy Spirit...*'[82] While the Great Commission contains no less than three basic parts, it begins with salvation or winning people to Christ. Their

---

[81] More Than Winning Presentation *DOWNLOAD*, at: http://fcaresources.com/promotional/more-winning-presentation-85-x-11

[82] Campus Crusade for Christ International at a Glance – Purpose, at: http://www.ccci.org/about-us/index.htm

The K.I.S.S. Principle

beliefs on this can be seen in their tract or information on, '*How to Know God Personally*.' The basic principles have been reprinted below:

How to Know God Personally

Principle 1:

God loves you and offers a wonderful plan for your life.

Principle 2:

All of us sin and our sin has separated us from God.

Principle 3:

Jesus Christ is God's only provision for our sin. Through Him we can know and experience God's love and plan for our life.

Principle 4:

We must individually receive Jesus Christ as Savior and Lord; then we can know and experience God's love and plan for our lives.

The following explains how you can receive Christ:

Rev. Clayton Hampton

You can receive Christ right now by faith through prayer

Prayer is talking to God. God knows your heart and is not so concerned with your words as He is with the attitude of your heart. The following is a suggested prayer:

"Lord Jesus, I need You. Thank You for dying on the cross for my sins. I open the door of my life and receive You as my Savior and Lord. Thank You for forgiving my sins and giving me eternal life. Take control of the throne of my life. Make me the kind of person You want me to be."[83]

As in the information shared concerning FCA, the information above reveals that the Campus Crusade for Christ lumps both salvation and service into what they consider a prayer for salvation. This becomes confusing for the person who is being led to the Lord for Salvation, because while they are being told that salvation is only by faith, they infer that the person must have Jesus *'...take control of the throne...'* of their life as a part of this experience in order to be *saved*.

---

[83] Campus Crusade for Christ International – How to Know God Personally, at: http://www.ccci.org/how-to-know-god/would-you-like-to-know-god-personally/index.htm

The K.I.S.S. Principle

Salvation according to InterVarsity Christian Fellowship

This organization, having begun in 1938 on the campus of the University of Michigan, is based on various university campuses and purposes '*...to establish and advance at colleges and universities witnessing communities of students and faculty who follow Jesus as Saviour and Lord: growing in love for God, God's Word, God's people of every ethnicity and culture and God's purposes in the world.*'[84]

While InterVarsity Press provides many books as resources concerning Evangelism, research concerning their position on Salvation has led us to the book called '*How to Give Away Your Faith*', by Paul Little. The path to this book within their information can be found in their document called, '*Resources for Training in Evangelism*', where point number 5 focuses on Witnessing, referencing this book as its resource for training.[85]

On pages 101-103 of his book, '*How to Give Away Your Faith*', Mr. Little provides a short list of five summarizations of what he refers to as, '*fairly easy to understand format*', of the gospel. In abbreviated form, they are:

---

[84] InterVarsity Christian Fellowhsip/USA – Our Purpose, at: http://www.intervarsity.org/about/our/our-purpose

[85] InterVarsity Evangelism – Resources For Training in Evangelism, at: http://www.intervarsity.org/evangelism/article_item.php?article_id=5452

Rev. Clayton Hampton

1. Three-Phase Pattern

   - Jesus' definition of what's wrong with people: They are separated from their Maker(Isaiah 53:6; Romans 3:11-12).

   - Jesus' diagnosis: Our disease of sin causes this separation (Mark 7:15).

   - Jesus' solution: Restore this relationship through his death (Romans 5:8; 1 Peter 2:24)

2. Four Steps to God

   - God: Twin facts—he is holy; he is the loving Creator (1 John 1:5; Psalm 100:3).

   - People: Twin tragedies—we have rebelled; we have broken God's law (James 2:10; Psalm 14:2-3).

   - Jesus Christ: He reconciled people to their Creator by his death (Romans 5:6-8).

   - Required response: Repent, believe, receive (Acts 17:30; John 1:12).

3. Jesus' Definition of Christianity

   - "I am the bread of life" (John 6:35).

The K.I.S.S. Principle

- "I am the way and the truth and the life" (John 14:6).

- "I am the light of the world" (John 8:12).

- "Come to me" (Matthew 11:28).

4. Religion versus Christianity

- Some believe Christianity is something you can do—that my good deeds must outweigh my bad deeds. They think, "If God grades on a curve, I'll get in" (Titus 3:5).

- The Bible says: "For it is by grace you have been saved, through faith—and this not from yourselves, it is the gift of God—not by works, so that no one can boast" (Ephesians 2:8-9).

- Christianity is something that has already been *done:* Only Jesus Christ can make us good enough to enter heaven. He forgives our sin and gives us his righteousness (Romans 5:8).

- The Bible says: "For we maintain that a man is justified by faith apart from observing the law" (Romans 3:28); "Therefore, since we have been justified through faith, we have peace

Rev. Clayton Hampton

with God through our Lord Jesus
Christ" (Romans 5:1).

5. Roman Road

- "All have sinned" (Romans 3:23).

- "The gift of God is eternal life"
  (Romans 6:23).

- "Believe in your heart...confess with
  your mouth" (Romans 10:9-10).[86]

According to Mr. Little, these summarizations should be used as are other concise summaries for a springboard to witnessing. He also goes further by cautioning against using religious terminology without explaining it to those we are talking with. For this, I applaud him, because it is too often that the religious community uses terminology they expect everyone to be familiar with when the fact is that most of society is Biblically illiterate. That being said, it should be noted that Mr. Little doesn't go into any real detail concerning the five summarizations printed above, as to what is meant or inferred by them or how to use them, what(if anything) should be emphasized and last of all what should be said to bring the person to the point of decision.

---

[86] How to Give Away Your Faith by Paul E. Little, Chapter 2 - What is Our Message?, Basic Pattern, pp. 101-103

The K.I.S.S. Principle

However, Mr. Little does go to some length, in the pages just prior to this information, talking about what he deems necessary for salvation. He appears to base his conclusion on his comparison of salvation to marriage, inferring that since marriage is not only about love between two parties, it is also a legal contract and is bound by the commitment of both parties, that salvation should be viewed in the same manner.

> "To get married, one finally has to come to a commitment of the will and say, 'I do,' committing himself to the other person and thereby establishing a relationship. It involves total commitment of intellect, emotions and will."[87]

In other words, and if the comparison holds true, according to Mr. Little, for a person to be saved or, that is, experience salvation, the individual needs to commit themselves to Christ completely. And yet, God says, salvation is a '...*gift*.' So, how does God's *gift*, that is accessed by *faith*, become a *commitment*, that is based on a *legal promise*? Well, basically, it happens because of man. In this case, Mr. Little, in his effort to make salvation or the gospel of salvation more understandable, not only made it more difficult to access, but actually changed it into something unlike the gospel. This type of action, though well meaning, needs to be

---

[87] How to Give Away Your Faith by Paul E. Little, Chapter 2 - What is Our Message?, 5. Becoming a Christian, p. 100

guarded against due to the consequences, as the Apostle Paul states:

> "*I marvel that ye are so soon removed from him that called you into the grace of Christ unto another gospel: Which is not another; but there be some that trouble you, and would pervert the gospel of Christ. But though we, or an angel from heaven, preach any other gospel unto you than that which we have preached unto you, let him be accursed.*" (Galatians 1:6-8)

So, the exhortation here is, '*...be careful*' to consider thoroughly what God has said about this great doctrine and keep it simple and clear.

Salvation according to The Navigators

The Navigators state that their 75-year-old slogan, "To Know Christ and To Make Him Know," aptly describes what Navigators do.

> As we befriend those who don't know Jesus or those just starting out in their relationship with Him, we show them how to grow, and how to help others grow, too.[88]

---

[88] The Navigators – What We Do, at: http://www.navigators.org/us/aboutus/what-we-do

The K.I.S.S. Principle

Simply put, they endeavor to fulfill the Great Commission. While it appears that their ministry is more focused on the last part of the Great Commission in discipling believers in an effort to assist the navigation of their life, they are also interested in leading people to Christ as well. The tool or format they use is called, '*The Bridge to Life*', the basics of which(without pictures/illustrations) are revealed below:

The Bridge to Life:

Step 1 God's Love and His plan
God Created us in His own image to be His friend and to experience a full life assured of his love, abundant and eternal.(John 10:10b; Romans 5:1)

Step 2 Our Problem: Separation from God
We chose to disobey god and go our own willful way. We still make this choice today. This results in separation from God.(Romans 3:23; Isaiah 59:2)

On our own, there's no way we can attain the perfection needed to bridge the gap to God. Through the ages,

Rev. Clayton Hampton

individuals have tried many ways---without success. (Proverbs 14:12)

Step 3 God's Remedy: The Cross
Jesus Christ is the only answer to this problem. He died on the cross and rose from the grave, paying the penalty for our sin and bridging the gap between God and people. (I Peter 3:18; I Timothy 2:5; Romans 5:8)

Step 4 Our Response
Believing means trust and commitment – acknowledging our sinfulness, trusting Christ's forgiveness and letting Him control our life. Eternal, abundant life is a gift for us to receive.(John 3:16; John 5:24)

How to receive Christ:

1. Admit your need(I am a sinner).

2. Be willing to turn from your sins(repent).

The K.I.S.S. Principle

3. Believe that Jesus Christ died for you an the cross and rose from the grave.

4. Through prayer, invite Jesus Christ to come in and control your life through the Holy Spirit(Receive Him as Lord and Savior of your life).

What to pray:

Dear Lord Jesus,

I know that I am a sinner and need Your forgiveness. I believe that You died for my sins. I want to turn from my sins. I now invite you to come into my heart and life. I want to trust and follow You as the Lord and Savior of my life.

In Your name. Amen.[89]

Actually, there are several groups that use this particular tool / illustration or some variation of it to lead people to Christ. It is therefore unfortunate that there are portions within it that appear to be disturbing. While much time could be taken here to elaborate on each area of concern, it is most disturbing to see their explanation in *Step 4 – Our Response*. The word translated as '...*believe*...' in John 3:16 is the Greek word

---

[89] The Navigators – The Bridge to Life, at: https://www.navigators.org/us/resources/illustrations/items/The%20Bridge%20to%20Life

πιστεύω, pronounced 'pē-styü'-ō'. It is translated 239 times as 'believe' and 4 or 5 times as 'commit'. Yet, they put a peculiar twist on the word by stating in Step 4 that *'Believing means **trust** and **commitment**...'* as opposed to stating that the word can be translated as **trust** or **commit**. They do this setting forth the idea that a person not only needs to *trust* in Christ's payment, but must also make a *commitment(or promise, or obligate)* to letting Christ control their life as the path to salvation, which appears to be more of an exchange than it does a gift, as described by Ephesians 2:8, 9. The word *commit* in this case appears to bear the meaning more along the line of *'...to place in trust or to entrust.'* In other words, the individual is *entrusting* their eternal destiny to Christ, due to His payment for them on the cross. This word does not appear to mean, *commitment*, as they infer the definition should be, meaning a promise or obligation to letting Christ control their life. While I believe that a person who has trusted in Christ as their Savior should desire to follow the Lord fervently, I don't believe that it is a requirement for salvation. As Ephesians 2:8 – 10 explains, we are not saved by our works, but unto good works.

Salvation according to Teen Challenge

Before delving into the Plan of Salvation as set forth by Teen Challenge, it would probably be a good idea to advise what Teen Challenge is and its mission/purpose. So, in their own words, they state:

The K.I.S.S. Principle

Mission Statement

To provide youth, adults and families with an effective and comprehensive Christian faith-based solution to life-controlling drug and alcohol problems in order to become productive members of society. By applying biblical principles, Teen Challenge endeavors to help people become mentally-sound, emotionally-balanced, socially-adjusted, physically-well, and spiritually-alive.[90]

The action or efforts of their mission statement is very admirable. But, in order to properly accomplish their goal, they need to lead the person to a saving knowledge of the Lord Jesus Christ. I found it extremely difficult to pinpoint this organizations beliefs on Salvation. Why, I don't know. Because you'd think that this would be something in the forefront of their information. However, I was able to locate a training resource they use called, *Sharing the Good News*, by Robert and Evelyn Bolton. The complete document is 209 pages and is used to train personnel how to lead people to Christ. But, the crux of their belief on salvation appears to be found in Lesson 8 of this publication called, *Explain the Way of Salvation* on pages 131-146, with the primary focus on pages 133-136, where they take their trainee through, what

---

[90] Teen Challenge USA, Mission Statement, at: http://teenchallengeusa.com/about/

Rev. Clayton Hampton

they call, the five steps of salvation. Initially, they make a valiant effort toward explaining salvation by focusing on what is probably the most simplified recording of the salvation experience in scripture, with the story of the salvation of the Philippian Jailor in Acts 16:19-34(*KJV*), recounted below:

Acts 16

[19] And when her masters saw that the hope of their gains was gone, they caught Paul and Silas, and drew *them* into the marketplace unto the rulers,

[20] And brought them to the magistrates, saying, These men, being Jews, do exceedingly trouble our city,

[21] And teach customs, which are not lawful for us to receive, neither to observe, being Romans.

[22] And the multitude rose up together against them: and the magistrates rent off their clothes, and commanded to beat *them*.

[23] And when they had laid many stripes upon them, they cast *them* into prison, charging the jailor to keep them safely:

The K.I.S.S. Principle

24 Who, having received such a charge, thrust them into the inner prison, and made their feet fast in the stocks.

25 And at midnight Paul and Silas prayed, and sang praises unto God: and the prisoners heard them.

26 And suddenly there was a great earth-quake, so that the foundations of the prison were shaken: and immediately all the doors were opened, and every one's bands were loosed.

27 And the keeper of the prison awaking out of his sleep, and seeing the prison doors open, he drew out his sword, and would have killed him-self, supposing that the prisoners had been fled.

28 But Paul cried with a loud voice, saying, Do thyself no harm: for we are all here.

29 Then he called for a light, and sprang in, and came trembling, and fell down before Paul and Silas,

30 And brought them out, and said, Sirs, what must I do to be saved?

Rev. Clayton Hampton

³¹ And they said, Believe on the Lord Jesus Christ, and thou shalt be saved, and thy house.

³² And they spake unto him the word of the Lord, and to all that were in his house.

³³ And he took them the same hour of the night, and washed *their* stripes; and was baptized, he and all his, straightway.

³⁴ And when he had brought them into his house, he set meat before them, and rejoiced, believing in God with all his house.

In reading this passage, you will note that Paul and Silas have been thrown into prison and are praying and singing at midnight, when an earthquake shakes the jail in such a manner that the cell doors open. The jailor, afraid for his life because of the possibility of the prisoners escaping, is ready to take his own life when Paul says, "*...we are all here. Do yourself no harm.*" He then enters their cell and asks Paul the big question, "*What must I do to be saved?*" To this, the Apostle Paul provides a brief and simple answer, "*Believe on the Lord Jesus Christ, and thou shalt be saved, and thy house.*" In the Teen Challenge training material that we are focusing on, they relate all of that information in its simplest form. Then, they confuse this

The K.I.S.S. Principle

clear presentation, given by Paul, with an unclear one of their own in the presentation of their The Five Steps:

Step 1: Acknowledge That You Are a Sinner – *Romans 3:23*

Step 2: Recognize That God Did Something About It – *John 3:16*

Step 3: Receive Christ as Your Savior – *Romans 6:23*

Step 4: Confess Sin and Get Rid of It – *I John 1:9*

Step 5: Confess and Believe That Jesus Is Savior and Lord – *Romans 10:9-10*[91]

I say that it is confusing, because I can see the process that the Philippian Jailor went through in the first three steps, as he accepts/receives Christ as his savior. But, I don't see either of their last two steps in the process. As a matter of fact in reference to Step 4, in I John 2:1 Paul tells us that he is writing to believers as he calls them, "*My little children...*" and not to the unsaved. That being said, it is easy enough to understand that John is

---

[91] Explain the Way of Salvation, Sharing the Good News by Robert and Evelyn Bolton, pages 133-146.

164

Rev. Clayton Hampton

not referring to the salvation experience in chapter 1, but instead of the fellowship of the believer with not only other believers, but with the Lord himself. And Step 5, in referring to the individual needing to "*Confess and Believe That Jesus Is Savior and Lord*" appears to be inferring that the person not only needs to accept Jesus as their Savior, but that they must make Him Lord or master of their life. As near as I can tell, v. 9 is talking about acknowledging who Jesus is, that he in fact is GOD! It isn't talking about making him the Lord or master of one's life.

That being said, do I believe that a person that has trusted in Christ as Savior should want to submit to Him as the Lord or master of their life? YES, I do! However, they are to do this NOT for a part of the purpose of obtaining Salvation, but in Service of the Lord that bought them with his own blood.

To say that they believe all five steps are necessary, is an understatement. On page 137, point #6 of the lesson in question, they advise:

> The pillars below represent the five steps of salvation which "build the bridge" from death to life.[92]

The diagram is not shown above, but they show "Death" on the left side of the diagram and "Life"

---

[92] Explain the Way of Salvation, point 6, Sharing the Good News by Robert and Evelyn Bolton, page 137

The K.I.S.S. Principle

on the right side of the diagram, with the five pillars left to right from Death to Life, indicating that one must complete *each pillar* in order(from left to right) to get to Life. Which according to them appears to mean that if the individual doesn't complete all of the steps, there is a gap in their salvation experience and they are not saved!

Salvation according to Youth for Christ

Youth for Christ is a non-profit organization that *appears* to focus on relationship evangelism, in an effort to reach youth via various programs located at middle school, high school and college campuses. The Metro Atlanta YFC states:

> Metro Atlanta Youth for Christ is committed to pursuing teenagers in their world, sharing with them the hope and love that God has for them. In pursuing teenagers, MAYFC will consistently strive to develop safe, bridge-building relationships with middle school and high school students through the different programs that we have to offer. As students come to know the hope and love that God has to offer, our belief is that a teenager's life will be impacted eternally.[93]

---

[93] Youth for Christ Atlanta, What We Do, at: http://www.atlantayfc.org/ministries/

While the Metro Atlanta YFC location has been cited above, most, if not all YFC organizations appear to hold to those same principles in reaching youth. While they do provide information on their Statement of Faith, concerning Salvation:

> We believe that, for the salvation of lost and sinful people, regeneration by the Holy Spirit is absolutely essential.[94]

They do not go into any great detail on their websites concerning Salvation and/or their approach to how they present it, except to say in the information contained on YFCJAM's website shown below:

How is evangelism done?

> *It takes boldness.* Let's face it. To share the message of Christ takes boldness. Even the Apostle Paul prayed for boldness to share the message of Christ. "Pray also for me, that whenever I open my mouth, words may be given me so that I will fearlessly make known the mystery of the gospel." (Eph.6:19)

> *It takes clarity.* The message of Christ is simple. Jesus died on the cross to pay the penalty for our sins. If we simply trust in what He did on the cross, then we receive the free gift of eternal life.

---

[94] Youth for Christ Atlanta, Statement of Faith, at: http://www.atlantayfc.org/about/statement_of_faith/

The K.I.S.S. Principle

> *It takes follow-up.* Once a person trusts in Jesus Christ as their Savior they need to be "discipled". This means that we help them grow in their knowledge of God and His Word.[95]

According to their focus above by YFC Jamaica, stating, "*It takes clarity*", it would appear that they are exactly correct! Yet, most all of the YFC websites will make reference to pointing youth to becoming a follower of Christ, which is admirable. But, they do not spend time providing an expanded view of what they share as the *Plan of Salvation* that would place a youth in God's family and make it possible for them to follow Christ.

Evangelistic
Salvation according to the American Bible Society

The American Bible Society is an organization that is focused not so much on presenting the various truths of scripture of which salvation is the main one, but primarily on the distribution of scripture worldwide so that others may have the opportunity to read the truths for themselves.

> Established in 1816, American Bible Society history follows closely and even intersects the history of our nation. In

---

[95] How is Evangelism Done?, Evangelism, YFC Jam, at: http://yfcjam.ning.com/page/evangelism-2

fact, ABS' early leadership reads like a Who's Who of patriots. Our first president was Elias Boudinot, former president of the Continental Congress. John Jay, John Quincy Adams, DeWitt Clinton and James Fennimore Cooper also played significant roles, as did Rutherford B. Hayes, Benjamin Harrison and Francis Scott Key. Since those early days, American Bible Society has worked closely with organizations to reach people in the United States and around the world who might otherwise not have access to a Bible.[96]

Salvation according to the American Tract Society

The American Tract Society began on May 11, 1825 stating their specific purpose was:

> To make Jesus Christ known in His redeeming grace and to promote the interests of vital godliness and sound morality, by the circulation of Religious Tracts, calculated to receive the approbation of all Evangelical Christians (from the ATS Statement of Purpose, 1825).[97]

---

[96] American Bible Society, About Us, at: http://www.americanbible.org/about/history

[97] American Tract Society, Early History of American Tract Society, at: http://www.atstracts.org/atshistory.html

The K.I.S.S. Principle

While the Plan of Salvation is the most important message in scripture, the way or manner of presentation and scriptures used in revealing it's message could be seen as varied as the number of Christian denominations that present it. While the ATS's purpose is to *make known* this great message, various denominations and individuals appear to have had a hand in the writing of the tracts that set forth that message. This simply means that the presentation of this message could and does vary from tract to tract depending on who wrote the tract, their training, and/or the denominational beliefs they hold to, etc.

According to the ATS Statement of Faith, they define salvation as:

> That the salvation of lost mankind is based solely on the finished work of Christ through regeneration by the Holy Spirit. Titus 3:4-7; Luke 24:46-47; Ephesians 2:8-9; John 14:6; Acts 4:12.[98]

I assume that all who write a salvation tract, published by the ATS, would have to hold to this belief. However, it is in the presentation of how it(salvation) is obtained that they may vary. Some of the tract authors are very well known, including Arthur DeMoss and Billy Graham. And even in those tracts the presentation varies somewhat.

---

[98] American Tract Society, ATS Vision, Mission, and Core Values, Statement of Faith, at: http://www.atstracts.org/atsvision.html

Rev. Clayton Hampton

Salvation according to Billy Graham Evangelistic Association

Since the 1940's, no one individual has had a greater impact on evangelizing the world than Billy Graham. The crusades held by him from the 1940's to present have brought countless numbers of people to Christ. However, it should be pointed out that while his efforts and accomplishments have appeared to be tremendous, the message of salvation, as he has presented it, hasn't been as clear as it could be. This can be seen in the tract written by him called, "Steps To Peace With God" the printed version of "Steps to Peace", provided on his website: http://stepstopeace.org/. The tract reveals four steps in the process, which basically holds to the same outline as many denominations:

Step 1 God's Purpose: Peace & Eternal Life
God loves you, and He wants you to live in peace with Him and to receive eternal life.(Romans 5:1; John 3:16; Romans 6:23b)

Step 2 Our Problem: Sin & Separation
God did not make us robots to mindlessly love and obey Him. Instead He gave us a will and freedom of choice.

But, like Adam, we often choose to disobey God and go our own selfish ways(read Genesis

171

The K.I.S.S. Principle

chapters 2-3). This side of our nature is called sin, and it separates us from God.(Romans 3:23, 6:23a; Genesis 3:23a)

Step 3 God's Remedy: The Cross
Jesus Christ is the only answer to this problem of separation from God. He died on the cross and rose from the grave to pay the penalty for our sin-completely bridging the gap between us and God.(Romans 5:8; Acts 4:12; I Timothy 2:5; John 5:24)

Step 4 Our Response: Receive Christ
We can receive Jesus Christ when we believe in His message and trust in Him alone to save us.(Acts 10:43; John 14:1; John 1:12)

This writer agrees with the aforementioned steps. What I have a problem with is the end of the tract where "How to Receive Christ" is explained:

How to Receive Christ

1. Admit your need(I am a sinner).

2. Be willing to turn from your sins(repent).

3. Believe that Jesus Christ died for you on the cross and rose from the grave.

4. Through prayer, invite Jesus Christ to come in and control your life through the Holy Spirit.(Receive Him as your Savior.)

Suggested Prayer:

Dear Lord Jesus, I know that I am a sinner, and I ask for Your forgiveness. I believe You died for my sins and rose from the dead. I turn from my sins and invite You to come into my heart and life. I want to trust and follow You as my Lord and Savior. In Your Name, amen.[99]

As has been explained in other portions of this book, this writer believes whole heartedly that Repentance is a vital part of the salvation experience. However, turning from sin and/or the willingness to do so is NOT Repentance, but an effort on the part of the individual to put them in a better place to accept the payment that Christ made on the cross for their sin. What this action does is change the free gift of God into an exchange process, where the individual agrees to change their life and accepts the payment of Christ for their sin. While the Greek word for repent in scripture is μετανοέω (*metanoeō*), which means "a change

---

[99] Steps to Peace, by Billy Graham, at: http://stepstopeace.org/

The K.I.S.S. Principle

of mind", where the individual changes their mind about who they are(a sinner) and that they stand in need of a savior, Jesus. When they come to understand this, they simply accept the payment that Christ made for their sin on the cross as their payment for their sin and receive the free gift of eternal life. Does God want us to not sin? Of course he does. However, this effort is accomplished with the help of the Holy Spirit after the person is saved, not as a part of the salvation experience.

Salvation according to Child Evangelism Fellowship

According to Child Evangelism Fellowship, the organization

> '...is a Bible-centered organization composed of born-again believers whose purpose is to evangelize boys and girls with the Gospel of the Lord Jesus Christ and to establish (disciple) them in the Word of God and in a local church for Christian living..'[100]

The focal point is reaching the every child with the Gospel of the Lord Jesus Christ. The important thing to know is what they mean by the word *Gospel*. So I have included a definition by them below:

---

[100] Child Evangelism Fellowship, About Us, at: http://www.cefonline.com/index.php?option=com_content&view=section&id=8&Itemid=100032

What is the Gospel?

Basically, "Gospel" means "good news". It refers to the good news of the death and resurrection of Jesus Christ.

1 Corinthians 15:1-4

Now, brothers, I want to remind you of the gospel I preached to you, which you received and on which you have taken your stand. **By this gospel you are saved**, if you hold firmly to the word I preached to you. Otherwise, you have believed in vain. For what I received I passed on to you as of first importance: that **Christ died for our sins** according to the Scriptures, that **he was buried**, that **he was raised on the third day** according to the Scriptures. (NIV)

To truly appreciate how the death and resurrection of Jesus can be considered "good news", we need to have a clear understanding of the following points:

1. God loves us.

The entire Bible is a love story; a true love story about how God created us and showered his love upon us. Even when we

The K.I.S.S. Principle

failed him and turned away from him, he never gave up on us.

1 John 4:9.10

This is how God showed his love to us: He sent his one and only Son into the world so that we could have life through him. This is what real love is: It is not our love for God; it is God's love for us. He sent his Son to die in our place to take away our sins.

2. God is holy.

God is perfectly pure, totally without sin.

Habakkuk 1:13a

Your eyes are too good to look at evil; you cannot stand to see those who do wrong.

1 Samuel 2:2a

There is no one holy like the Lord.

3. We are not holy.

We have all done things that are wrong. We have all sinned.

Romans 3:23

Everyone has sinned and fallen short of God's glorious standard.

4. Our "unholiness", our sin separates us from God.

Isaiah 59:2

It's your sins that have cut you off from God. Because of your sins, he has turned away and will not listen anymore. (NLT)

5. God's answer to this problem of separation was Jesus.

John 3:16

God loved the world so much that he gave his one and only Son so that

whoever believes in him may not be lost, but have eternal life.

6. Jesus died on the cross, was buried, and on the 3rd day, rose again.

The K.I.S.S. Principle

Jesus took the punishment for our sins so that we can be made holy.

1 Peter 3:18

Christ himself suffered for sins once. He was not guilty, but he suffered for those who are guilty to bring you to God. His body was killed, but he was made alive in the spirit.

Romans 4:25

Jesus was given to die for our sins, and he was raised from the dead to make us right with God.

7. We don't have to remain separated from God anymore.

Because of Jesus' death and resurrection, we can be reconciled to God if we:

Admit that we have sinned and ask God to forgive us

A. Believe that Jesus died on the cross to be punished instead of us, and

B. Invite Jesus into our lives to help us turn away from sin

John 1:12

But to all who did accept him and believe in him he gave the right to become children of God.

1 John 1:9

But if we confess our sins, he will forgive our sins, because we can trust God to do what is right. He will cleanse us from all the wrongs we have done.

3. **We can be assured of a place in heaven.**

Once we have put our faith in Jesus our sins are forgiven and our relationship with God is restored. We are assured of a place in heaven – a perfect place without sickness, pain or hunger. In heaven, everyone is perfectly happy.

Rev 21:4a

He will wipe away every tear from their eyes, and there will

The K.I.S.S. Principle

be no more death, sadness, crying, or pain.

Rev 21:21

The twelve gates were twelve pearls, each gate having been made from a single pearl. And the street of the city was made of pure gold as clear as glass.

4. Jesus is the only way.

There is no other way for us to restore our relationship with God, no other way for us to get to heaven.

John 14:6

Jesus answered, "I am the way, and the truth, and the life. The only way to the Father is through me.

5. This restoration is God's gift to us.

God extends this gift to all even though we do not deserve it. All this is by the grace of God.

Ephesians 2:8,9

Rev. Clayton Hampton

> I mean that you have been saved
> by grace through believing. You
> did not save yourselves; it was
> a gift from God. It was not the
> result of your own efforts, so
> you cannot brag about it.[101]

As is the case in most all of the varied points of view concerning salvation, this writer can agree with most of the points revealed here except one. To prevent the need of going back and forth to the point in question to compare it with my evaluation, I have reprinted it below:

> 6. We don't have to remain separated
>   from God anymore.
>
>   Because of Jesus' death and
>   resurrection, we can be recon-
>   ciled to God if we:
>
>   Admit that we have sinned and
>   ask God to forgive us
>
>   A. Believe that Jesus died on
>   the cross to be punished
>   instead of us, and
>
>   B. Invite Jesus into our lives to
>   help us turn away from sin

---

[101] What is the Gospel, Child Evangelism Resources, at: http://www.letthe-littlechildrencome.com/child-evangelism-resources/what-is-the-gospel/

The K.I.S.S. Principle

To evaluate this properly, we should state that the previous six points have stated:

1. **God loves us.**

2. **God is holy.**

3. **We are not holy.**

4. **Our "unholiness", our sin separates us from God.**

5. **God's answer to this problem of separation was Jesus.**

6. **Jesus died on the cross, was buried, and on the 3rd day, rose again.**

These points tell us that God loves us and is holy. We are not holy and its our unholiness(or sin) that separates us from God. But, that God has an answer to that issue in Jesus, because He was completely holy and died to make the required payment for our sin. Now according to this organization, the steps to repairing that separation is found in sub points A – C under main point 7. Sub point A is very important, because if an individual doesn't admit or recognize that they are a sinner, then they will not see a need for a savior. Sub point B is the acknowledgement of the solution to their problem in Sub point A. However, Sub point C, while it is common phraseology or terminology in several denominations, doesn't really explain

Rev. Clayton Hampton

what needs to be done at this point and thus needs more explanation. The phrase sounds good, but what does it mean? To this writer it doesn't appear to be focusing on the salvation experience, but more on the experience of a dedicated believer trying to live a life that is honoring and glorifying unto the Lord. If that is, in fact, the gist of the phrase, then it is actually not talking about salvation, but about the life of a Christian after they have been saved. What the person needs to do at this point is *accept(by faith) the payment that Christ made on the cross for their sin as their payment for their sin.* That is salvation!

Salvation according to Gideons International

Before elaborating on this organizations beliefs concerning salvation it should be pointed out that this is an Interdenominational Organization. In other words, it is made up of many members of different denominations. While all of the members believe in Christ, their particular views concerning the plan of salvation may differ. Their focus and/ or goal is to make God's Word(The Bible) available to everyone. Thus, you find it placed in the hands of anyone ready to receive a copy. When an individual isn't available, a copy may have been placed in a hotel room making it available to them. That being said, how do they seek to bring people to Christ? According to their home website, they believe that a person becomes a Christian by:

Become a Christian

The K.I.S.S. Principle

Many people are looking for God. If you're one of those people, we'd like to share with you that the Bible has what you are seeking. It contains answers to life's vital questions, and—most important—can help you understand how to have a right relationship with God. Here are some selected verses:

God Loves You

For God so loved the world, that he gave his only begotten Son, that whosoever believeth in him should not perish, but have everlasting life. —John 3:16

But God commendeth his love towards us, in that, while we were yet sinners, Christ died for us. —Romans 5:8

All Are Sinners

For all have sinned, and come short of the glory of God. —Romans 3:23

As it is written, There is none righteous, no, not one. —Romans 3:10

God's Remedy for Sin

For the wages of sin is death; but the gift of God is eternal life through Jesus Christ our Lord. —Romans 6:23

But as many as received him, to them gave he power to become the sons of God, even to them that believe on his name. —John 1:12

All May Be Saved Now

Behold, I stand at the door, and knock: if any man hear my voice, and open the door, I will come in to him. — Revelation 3:20(a)

For whosoever shall call upon the name of the Lord shall be saved. — Romans 10:13

But these are written, that ye might believe that Jesus is the Christ, the Son of God; and that believing ye might have life through his name. —John 20:31

Receive Christ as Your Savior Now... Pray the Following Prayer

Confessing to God that I am a sinner, and believing that the Lord Jesus Christ died for my sins on the cross and was raised for my justification, I now receive and confess Him as my personal Savior.[102]

---

[102] The Gideon's International, How to Become a Christian, at: http://www.gideons.org/BecomeAChristian/BecomeAChristian.aspx

The K.I.S.S. Principle

I applaud their use of scripture, but sometimes as we know, people jump around all over scripture and never get to the point that they really need to direct people to. And, it would behoove anyone when using scripture to discuss or talk about salvation to ensure that the passages they use are salvation passages and not passages that are talking about something else. In the case of the information that has been quoted from their website here, one scripture doesn't really belong. Rev. 3:20 has been, and is used by many people as a salvation verse or passage, but it is not talking about eternal salvation. In this verse, the Lord is talking to the Church of Laodicea and advising them that while they think that they are serving Him properly, they are in fact, luke warm in their service and that He is a chastening God. But, that being said, that He has an open door for contact with them to mend their relationship with Him, if they are willing. This is not about eternal salvation, but about mending their relationship with the Lord. They(The Gideons) do not appear to go into any detail regarding what the *original meaning* of some of the important/key words are in the scriptures, to enlighten the individual so that they will know exactly what to do. When using Biblical words and/or terminology, it is very important to remember that while believers may understand what is being said, that the unbeliever most of the time doesn't understand. Therefore, it is important for the individual who is using said words and/or terminology to enlighten them. Please understand that I am not saying that you shouldn't use Biblical words and/or

Rev. Clayton Hampton

terminology. But, I am saying that if you are going to use them, do the unbeliever, yourself and the Lord a favor and explain them.

Salvation according to The Gospel Coalition

In the event that you are unfamiliar with The Gospel Coalition, the organization defines itself in the following manner:

The Gospel for All of Life: Preamble

> We are a fellowship of evangelical churches deeply committed to renewing our faith in the gospel of Christ and to reforming our ministry practices to conform fully to the Scriptures. We have become deeply concerned about some movements within traditional evangelicalism that seem to be diminishing the church's life and leading us away from our historic beliefs and practices. On the one hand, we are troubled by the idolatry of personal consumerism and the politicization of faith; on the other hand, we are distressed by the unchallenged acceptance of theological and moral relativism. These movements have led to the easy abandonment of both biblical truth and the transformed living mandated by our historic faith. We not only hear of these influences, we see their effects. We have committed

The K.I.S.S. Principle

> ourselves to invigorating churches with new hope and compelling joy based on the promises received by grace alone through faith alone in Christ alone.[103]

According to this statement, their efforts appear to be commendable. However, that being said, their position regarding Salvation appears to fall under the guise of many who, while they appear to hold to a conservative doctrinal position regarding the existence of sin, it's penalty and the payment provided by Christ to allow sinner's forgiveness and entrance into Heaven fail to properly evaluate and/or define the word *repent* as they provide an explanation of what a person needs to do to be saved:

> ...what are we to do to be saved? We must turn to God in Christ, which entails turning back from sin. If we *repent* of (decide to forsake and turn from) our sin (as best we understand it) and *trust* in Christ as a living person, we will be saved from God's righteous wrath against our sins.[104]

What this interpretation and/or definition causes is a contradiction between scripture and their way of Salvation. For, to *turn from* or *back from* *sin* is an effort on the part of man to put him in

---

[103] The Gospel Coalition – Who We Are: http://thegospelcoalition.org/about/who

[104] God's Plan of Salvation at: http://thegospelcoalition.org/pdf-articles/plan_salvation.pdf

a position of gaining God's favor for the purpose of salvation. Quite simply put, this action constitutes *works* on the behalf of the individual. As has already been stated in other portions of this book, the proper definition of the word/action *repent* is 'a change of mind'. When a person repents, they are, in fact, changing their mind from not believing and/or trusting in Christ's payment(in this case) to trusting in His completed payment on the cross as their payment for their sin. This action clears the person of the debt/payment for sin, *death* and places them in a position of being justified before God and able to go to Heaven.

Family
Salvation according to Awana Clubs

The Awana Clubs are an independent youth organization whose name is based upon its focal verse:

> Study to shew thyself *approved* unto God, a *workman* that needeth *not* to be *ashamed*, rightly dividing the word of truth.
>
> II Timothy 2:15
>
> **A**pproved **W**orkmen **A**re **N**ot **A**shamed!

The organization, while independent, is utilized by many denominations as the main youth ministry of their churches to reach youth in or near their church with the gospel, which they explain as:

The K.I.S.S. Principle

God's Offer of Forgiveness and an Eternal Future in Heaven

I am a sinner.

Sin is anything contrary to the nature of God. Every person is born a sinner, and every person commits sin. God is holy and hates sin. Because He is just, He must punish sin. The punishment for sin is eternal separation from God.

God's Word says: *... all have sinned ... (Romans 3:23); For the wages of sin is death...(Romans 6:23a)*.

I am incapable of saving myself.

Because I am born in sin, no action of mine can accomplish anything toward my salvation. I cannot get to heaven by being good, attending church, praying or anything else. I am helpless and unable to make myself worthy of heaven.

God says: *Not by [good works] which we have done, but according to His mercy He saved us...(Titus 3:5a)*.

Only God can save me because only God is sinless.

God gave His Son, Jesus Christ, to be my Savior by paying the penalty of death for my sin in my place.

But God commendeth His love toward us, in that, while we were yet sinners, Christ died for us. (Romans 5:8)

My salvation was accomplished on the cross.

Jesus paid for all my sin by dying, shedding His blood and rising from the grave. His blood paid my penalty. His resurrection defeated death. He is now in heaven, interceding for me before God.

For Christ also hath once suffered for sins, the just for the unjust, that He might bring us to God…(1 Peter 3:18a).

I can only be saved by trusting that what Jesus Christ did on the cross is sufficient to save me.

Believing is trusting what God did for me. I can add nothing to my salvation. When I believe that His death was a complete payment for me, He gives me eternal life.

…Believe on the Lord Jesus Christ, and thou shalt be saved…(Acts 16:31)

The K.I.S.S. Principle

*He that believeth on the Son hath ever-
lasting life: and he that believeth not the
Son shall not see life; but the wrath of
God abideth on him. (John 3:36)*

**Once I am saved, I am saved
for eternity.**

Once saved, I cannot lose my salvation.
No creature or thing can take it away
from me. I cannot lose it by any action
of my own.

God says:.... *I give unto them eternal life;
and they shall never perish. (John 10:28)*

*For God so loved the world, that He gave
His only begotten Son, that whosoever
believeth in Him should not perish, but
have everlasting life. (John 3:16)*[105]

It may sound amazing at this point, due to the com-
ments that this writer has made concerning other
plans for, or of salvation provided in this communication, but I agree completely with their view.
While the information above doesn't delve into the
Greek words that were translated into the English,
it does take the opportunity to explain what is actually meant by what is stated in the passages. This

---

[105] Awana Clubs, God's Offer of Forgiveness and an Eternal Future in
Heaven, at: http://awana.org/youcanhaveeternallife/you-can-have-
eternal-life.default.pg.html

is an important part of helping the unbeliever not only understand what Christ has done for them, but what is expected of them with regard to what must be done for them to appropriate salvation and be assured that they are going to Heaven when they die.

Salvation according to Focus on the Family

This organization's thrust is basically defined by it's name, where the goal is to help or assist families thrive:

Helping Families Thrive

Focus on the Family is a global Christian ministry dedicated to helping families thrive. We provide help and resources for couples to build healthy marriages that reflect God's design, and for parents to raise their children according to morals and values grounded in biblical principles.[106]

However, according to their *Guiding Principles*, their primary reason for existence '...*is to spread the Gospel of Jesus Christ through a practical outreach to homes'.*[107] This brings us to the question of what do they believe concerning eternal Salvation

---

[106] Focus on the Family, About Us, Helping Families Thrive, at: http://www. focusonthefamily.com/about_us.aspx

[107] Focus on the Family, Guiding Principles, at: http://www. focusonthefamily.com/about_us/guiding-principles.aspx

The K.I.S.S. Principle

and/or how is it attained? I have always regarded *Focus on the Family* as a scripturally based organization, and still do. However, their presentation of the gospel in the information I obtained online left me perplexed and I am a Christian. In viewing all of the information provided by the various entities and/or denominations, churches or organizations, etc. I have tried to review each presentation of the gospel as though I were an unbeliever. In my observation herein, I would have to say that not only was I disappointed, but that I was confused. I do not see an unbeliever reviewing this information and getting *saved.* As a matter of fact, I don't believe that they would read through the information completely. My final comment on this is to simply say that if their primary reason for existence is to spread the Gospel of Jesus Christ through a practical outreach to homes, I hope that they have a shorter and easier to understand presentation of this great message than that which is presented in the displays on their website. From my personal review of this information, the closest the organization comes to presenting the Gospel is in a section called *Christ and the Good News*, where they discuss the fact that the good news is that Christ died for us:

Christ and the Good News

But Christ's death and resurrection do not automatically accomplish a restored relationship between us and God. We must respond personally, sincerely and with a commitment to turn away from our sin (repent), acknowledging that only Christ can save us from our fallen condition.

The *gospel or "good news"* is that Christ has died for us, meaning that we can ask for His forgiveness and receive it. There is no magic in this request or exact ritual we must follow. It is simply a matter of turning to God through Christ and, through prayer, confessing that we have fallen short of His standards, expressing our desire to have Christ direct our lives for His glory, not ours. [2][108]

[2] "Steps to Peace with God," by the Billy Graham Evangelistic Association, presents the gospel message clearly and simply, outlining "God's Purpose," "The Problem," "God's Bridge," and "Our Response."

Please note that they confuse the issue by their explanation of what a person must do to experience salvation in stating, "*We must respond personally, sincerely and with a commitment to turn away from our sin (repent)...*" If they had provided

---

[108] Focus on the Family, Restoring Our Relationship With God, Christ and the Good News, at: http://www.focusonthefamily.com/faith/becoming_a_christian/how_can_i_be_saved/restoring_our_relationship_with_god.aspx

The K.I.S.S. Principle

a proper interpretation of the word "repent" this might have been okay. Remember that the word "repent"(Greek metaneo) means to "change your mind". So, if they were saying that you need to be sincere about changing your mind concerning Christ, who you are(a sinner) and what you must do(accept the payment Christ made for you on the cross as your payment for your sin), then yes, they would be correct. And, does God want us to discontinue our sinning, yes He does. But, that is a part of our service to the Lord in our walk with Christ as we become more like Him. You will also note that the reference they make in the previous display[2] is to a tract called *Steps to Peace with God*, by the Billy Graham Evangelistic Association, that was evaluated earlier in this book(page 113). They state in the revealed information above that this tract "*...presents the gospel message clearly and simply...*". But, by reviewing the information provided on this tract, you will note that this is not as true as it may seem. For more information on that tract, please review that section of this book.

Salvation according to Promise Keepers

According to the Promise Keepers Core Values:

> Promise Keepers is a Christ-centered organization dedicated to motivating men to influence their world through a relationship with Jesus Christ. The key to Promise Keepers are individual men keeping their promises in the context

of their family, church and community. Promise Keepers is dedicated to calling men into the ongoing process of godliness. When we reach men, we reach families.

This organization appears to be a discipleship oriented group that focuses on its members holding to the 7 Promises it sets forth as its primary purpose, seen below:

7 Promises

PROMISE 1

A Promise Keeper is committed to honoring Jesus Christ through worship, prayer and obedience to God's Word in the power of the Holy Spirit.(Romans 12:1-2 Also see: Psalm 95:1-7; 98:2-3, Proverbs 3:5-6, Jeremiah 3:3-13, Luke 18:1 John 4:32, Acts 2:30-39, Romans 12:1-3, 1 Corinthians 6:19, Galatians 2:20, 1 Thessalonians 1:6-10, 2 Timothy 3:16, Hebrews 12:1-11, 2 Peter 3:11, Revelation 4:8-11)

PROMISE 2

A Promise Keeper is committed to pursuing vital relationships with a few other men, understanding that he needs brothers to help him keep

The K.I.S.S. Principle

his promises.(Ecclesiastes 4:12 Also see: Genesis 14:12-16, Job 16:1-5, Proverbs 17:17;27:17, Ecclesiastes 4:9-11, Matthew 4:18-22, Mark 14:32-34, Luke 6:12-16, Acts 20:32-38, Romans 15:30-33, Colossians 4:7-9, James 5:16, 1 Peter 5:4-10, Hebrews 10:24, 3 John 3-4)

PROMISE 3

A Promise Keeper is committed to practicing spiritual, moral, ethical, and sexual purity. (Hebrews 4:15-16 Also see: Exodus 20:3; 33:12-17, Joshua 7:6-12, 1 Kings 11:1-12, 1 Chronicles 29:17-18, Psalm 101:2-4, Proverbs 11:1; 19:5; 20:11, Ecclesiastes 7:11-12, Song of Songs 2:4-7; 7:1-13, Micah 6:6-8, Matthew 4:1-11, Romans 16:19, 1 Peter 2:11-22)

PROMISE 4

A Promise Keeper is committed to building strong marriages and families through love, protection and biblical values.(Ephesians 5:25; 6:4 Also see: Genesis 2:22-25, Deuteronomy 6:1-9, Ezra 9:12, Esther 2:10-11, Job 1:1-5, Psalm 127:1-5, Proverbs 5:15-20; 17:6, Proverbs 18:22; 22:15, Proverbs 31:10-31, Song of Songs 2:1; 4:1-7,

Song of Songs 5:16; 8:6-7; 8:13-14, Joel 1:2-3, Mark 10:6-9, Acts 16:14-15 Hebrews 13:4)

PROMISE 5

A Promise Keeper is committed to supporting the mission of his church by honoring and praying for his pastor, and by actively giving his time and resources. (1 Timothy 5:17 See also: Genesis 45:8, Malachi 3:10, Matthew 25:14-30, Luke 14:26-27, John 17:15-19, Acts 4:32-37; 5:12, Acts 6:1-5; 11:29-30; 28:7-10, Romans 12:4-8, 2 Corinthians 9:6-15, Galatians 6:3-6, Philippians 4:10-18, Hebrews 10:25, 1 Peter 2:4-5; 4:8-11)

PROMISE 6

A Promise Keeper is committed to reaching beyond any racial and denominational barriers to demonstrate the power of biblical unity. (John 17:20-21 See also Genesis 11:1-8, Leviticus 19:32-34, Numbers 25:1-18, Ruth 1:16-17, Psalm 13:31; 199:63, Proverbs 6:1-35; 22:2, Isaiah 53:1-12, Luke 10:25-37, Acts 10:24-33, 1 Corinthians 1:10-17; 3:3-9, Ephesians 2:14; 4:2-3, Revelation 5:9; 7:9; 14:65)

PROMISE 7

The K.I.S.S. Principle

> A Promise Keeper is committed to influencing his world, being obedient to the Great Commandment (see Mark 12:30-31) and the Great Commission (Matthew 28:19-20 See also Exodus 1:15-27, Nehemiah 2:17-20; 5:14-18, Psalm 82:3-4, Proverbs 1:1-6; 19:17; 28:27, Matthew 7:15-20, Mark 12:30-31, Acts 5:38-39, Romans 10:14, Corinthians 9:19-23, 2 Corinthians 9:6-11, 1 Thessalonians 4:9-10, 2 John 4-6).[109]

Promise 7 is the focal point for discussion. They appear to be committed to the *Great Commission*. However, they do not go into any detail on the message they convey to prospective believers. This may be because Promise Keepers reaches across denominational lines and therefore leaves the presentation of the Gospel or Good News to the individual based upon their denominational beliefs. If this is true, then the organization is more of an interfaith or interdenominational group. My personal opinion is that they should have one more promise or that is a Promise 8 that states that "A Promise Keeper is committed to keeping the plan of salvation and its presentation clear as it is presented in scripture."

---

[109] Promise Keepers, 7 Promises, at: http://www.promisekeepers.org/about/7-promises

Rev. Clayton Hampton

<u>Missions & Outreach</u>
Salvation according to Habitat For Humanity

On the surface, the average individual may think of *Habitat for Humanity* as a completely humanitarian organization that supports those in need by assisting in providing shelters or housing for them. However they define their organization as:

> We are a nonprofit, ecumenical <u>Christian ministry</u> founded on the conviction that every man, woman and child should have a decent, safe and affordable place to live. We build with people in need regardless of race or religion. We welcome volunteers and supporters from all backgrounds.[110]

So, in their own words, they are an *ecumenical Christian Ministry*. They go on to say they are a Christian Ministry that is involved in interfaith projects. While this organization appears to accomplish a great many good things across the board with what they, with the assistance of other faiths, provide for those in need regarding housing, the manner in which this is accomplished causes them to appear not as a Christian organization, but more humanitarian. The organization appears to use the principals of scripture without the message of scripture. The thrust of their organization appears to be in their effort to:

---

[110] Habitat for Humanity, Who We Are, at: http://www.habitat.org/how

The K.I.S.S. Principle

> ...mobilize the faith community to build houses as a tangible expression of God's love.[111]

Yes, God loves us, but not just so that we can experience a decent life here. He wants us to spend an eternity with Him, which is appropriated by our faith in Christ's death on the cross as our payment for our sin. This is salvation and reveals the most tangible expression of God's love in the giving of His Son to pay for our sin.

Salvation according to New Tribes Mission

New Tribes Mission is an organization that began in 1942 by Paul Fleming and five others that has as its goal that...*of reaching people who have no access to the Gospel.*[112] Their effort to accomplish their goal is seen in their ministering among unreached people groups worldwide, working in the tribal culture and language to present foundational Bible teaching and eventually establish mature churches. Their ***Statement of Faith*** reveals:

> 5. That the Lord Jesus Christ shed His blood and died as a sacrifice for the sins of the whole world.

---

[111] Habitat for Humanity, Building on Faith, Event possibilities, at: http://www.habitat.org/cr/bof.aspx

[112] New Tribes Mission, Our Heritage, at: http://usa.ntm.org/our-heritage

6. That salvation is a free and everlasting gift of God, entirely apart from works, received by personal faith in the Lord Jesus Christ.[113]

Getting to the point where a NTM missionary is in a position to present the gospel to the people group they are ministering to can be a long intense task. However, the manner in which they make that presentation as well as the message they convey is very true to scripture and therefore very uncomplicated, as their YouTube recording reveals:

http://www.youtube.com/watch?v=htlex Enz4hQ[114]

You will note, by watching the video in its entirety, that the missionary only told the stories from scripture as presented in scripture and did not bring into the session any denominational jargon, language, etc. that might confuse the people they were ministering to. The result of their presentation was that most all of the people group trusted in Christ as their Savior, Praise the Lord!

Salvation according to the Salvation Army

Most everyone is familiar with the organization called the Salvation Army. They are recognized

---

[113] New Tribes Mission, What We Believe, Statement of Faith, at: http://usa.ntm.org/what-we-believe

[114] New Tribes Mission, Ee-taow: The Story of Mark Zook-Missions, at: http://www.youtube.com/watch?v=htlexEnz4hQ

The K.I.S.S. Principle

for their humanitarian efforts in meeting the needs of the poor. But, for most, you probably think of them especially at Christmas time, when you see a Santa Claus standing next to a collection/donation pot outside a store. According to their own words, however, they state their mission is two-fold, in their statement:

> The Salvation Army, an international movement, is an evangelical part of the universal Christian church. Its message is based on the Bible. Its ministry is motivated by the love of God. Its mission is to preach the gospel of Jesus Christ and to meet human needs in His name without discrimination.[115]

The link to their website:

What We Believe:
http://www.salvationarmyusa.org/usn/
what-we-believe

while it doesn't provide, what would be known as, a plan of salvation, does provide information on what they believe about attaining and keeping salvation in the form of a Doctrinal Statement. While most of the information displayed in this information appears to fall in line with the doctrinal statements of most conservative Christian beliefs, there

---

[115] The Salvation Army, Our Mission, at: http://www.salvationarmyusa.org/usn/about

Rev. Clayton Hampton

is one point(point 9 of their Doctrinal Statement) that concerns me:

> **9. We believe** that continuance in a state of salvation depends upon continued obedient faith in Christ.[116]

This statement appears to infer that if an individual doesn't adhere to what is set forth in this point, then that the individual has lost their salvation and/or is no longer saved! This is just not in accord with scriptural teaching on eternal security, because the Lord assures us that we are eternally secure in Christ in John 6:37, 39; 10:27-29. Then, He goes on to say that our eternal salvation isn't dependent on our hold on Him, but on His hold on us, I Peter 1:5. Put simply, the person they appear to be placing their faith in doesn't appear to be the Jesus of the Bible, or they do not believe what the Bible teaches on salvation and the security of the believer. After much deliberation concerning this, I contacted one of the Salvation Army locations and spoke with a representative there on the matter. They confirmed that the statement was passed down to their organization via Mr. William Booth, their founder, who was an ordained Methodist Minister, and therefore obtained his beliefs from Methodist teachings that originated with Armenian beliefs on the matter. In short, they believe that an individual can be saved, and then lose their

---

[116] The Salvation Army, What We Believe, at: http://www.salvationarmyusa.org/usn/what-we-believe

salvation, if they are not persistent or do not continue in "*...obedient faith in Christ.*" That being said, *if their belief/statement were true*, it would mean that there would be no need for God's discipline of His children taught in Hebrews 12. I say that, because by their statement or belief, a person would either be saved and serving the Lord or they would be lost. There would never be a case where a person was saved and yet at the same time out of God's will, etc. and in need of God's discipline. They are not teaching salvation from sin for eternity, but probation from the penalty of sin as long as they are obedient to faith in Christ.

Salvation according to Jews for Jesus

As in the case of most all of groups being discussed in this book, I am certain that a fair amount of time could be used discussing this organization, but suffice it to say that in accord with the organizations statement about itself,

> "Our name tells who we are, who we stand for and what we do."[117]

Originally, Jews for Jesus began as a slogan in the late 1960s, then was founded as an organization by Moishe Rosen officially in September of 1973, who revolutionized the evangelistic methods and materials of the group with a creative approach to

---

[117] Jews for Jesus, A Brief History of Jews for Jesus, at: https://www.jewsforjesus.org/about/timeline/history

sharing the gospel. The efforts of the group are to reach people with the gospel, specifically or especially the Jewish community. With regard to their belief or teaching on salvation or getting saved, it can be seen in their publication/document called, "Knowing God", below:

Knowing God

No one can ever get saved by the mere click of a button. But you can get saved by believing God's word and receiving His free gift of salvation in Y'shua, Jesus the Messiah. Here are four statements from the Bible that you need to believe in and agree to in order to get saved.

1. The Bible says:

"The LORD looks down from heaven upon the children of men, to see if there are any who understand, who seek God. They have all turned aside, they have together become corrupt; [There is] none who does good, No, not one" (Psalm 14:2-3). "For all have sinned and fall short of the glory of God" (Romans 3:23).

"I agree with the Bible and admit before God that I am a sinner. I do not meet God's standard of goodness. I know that I can never be good enough on my own."

The K.I.S.S. Principle

2. The Bible says:

"But your iniquities have separated you from your God; And your sins have hidden [His] face from you, So that He will not hear" (Isaiah 59:2). "For the wages of sin [is] death, but the gift of God [is] eternal life in Messiah Jesus our Lord" (Romans 6:23).

"I agree with the Bible and believe that because I am a sinner I am separated from God. I deserve the punishment of death and need God's forgiveness and His gift of eternal life."

3. The Bible says:

"But He [was] wounded for our transgressions, [He was] bruised for our iniquities; The chastisement for our peace [was] upon Him, And by His stripes we are healed" (Isaiah 53:5). "But God demonstrates His own love toward us, in that while we were still sinners, Messiah died for us" (Romans 5:8).

"I agree with the Bible and believe that Jesus the Messiah died to pay the penalty for my sins."

4. The Bible says:

> "If you confess with your mouth the Lord Jesus and believe in your heart that God has raised Him from the dead, you will be saved." (Romans 10:9) "But as many as received Him, to them He gave the right to become children of God, to those who believe in His name." (John 1:12)
>
> **DO YOU agree with the Bible and believe that Jesus rose again from the dead? Are you now prepared to confess Him as your Lord, believe in His name and receive Him as your Savior?**
>
> **Yes|No**
>
> If you don't understand or don't agree with these four points and would like to discuss this with someone click here.[118]

While, for the most part, I do agree with the information provided here, the invitation question at the end appeared to be a little confusing. I say that, because of the first segment of the question that states, "*Are you now prepared to confess Him as your Lord?*" While to a Christian, this may seem like a logical question, it is important for Christians to remember/assume that the unsaved/unbelieving

---

[118] Jews for Jesus, Knowing God, at: http://www.jewsforjesus.org/contact/get-saved/knowing-god

The K.I.S.S. Principle

community does not know or understand Biblical terminology or what the group believes the said terminology means! After going back and forth with a representative of Jews for Jesus several times, via email, it was determined that the word/term **Lord** used in their question is a direct reference to who Jesus is, that He is, in fact, God. This is because only God could/would be perfect enough to completely pay for sin. I agree with this information, but still believe that more could/should be stated to provide a clearer understanding of the salvation experience and exactly what is required of the individual regarding it.

Salvation according to Operation Mobilization

This worldwide ministry began as the faithful prayer of an American housewife, Dorothea Clapp, for the students of her high school in the 1950s. She eventually gave the gospel of John to one of her students, George Verwer, who later surrendered his life to the Lord for service at a Billy Graham meeting. Between George Verwer and two of his friends in college, their concerns and prayers were brought to fruition in beginning a new ministry reaching out to many lost people around the world now known as Operation Mobilization.[119] As to what the organization currently believes regarding salvation, one of their core values is

---

[119] OM International, The History of OM, at: http://www.om.org/en/about/history

"Evangelizing the world" and according to their Statement of Faith, "We believe that man is saved through repentance and faith in the finished work of Christ. Justification is through grace alone."[120] While these statements are admirable, they do not completely answer the question at hand.

In an effort to expand on this and answer the question of salvation and/or how it is presented by Operation Mobilization, I decided to email them for a more detailed response concerning this. The response I received, displayed below, was somewhat vague, but did provide an indication as to why no specific answer could be given:

> Because OM is an international, inter-denominational, intercultural global ministry, we don't have one set way of presenting the gospel or leading people in a prayer of salvation. This means that within OM there are a variety of ways of presenting the gospel. There can also be disagreements within OM on how to define repentance, as well as on matters like leading people in a sinner's prayer, just as there are disagreements within US evangelicalism on the definitions and methods.[121]

---

[120] OM International, What We Believe, Core Values/Statement of Faith: http://www.om.org/en/about/what-we-believe

[121] OM International, Partnership with Ministries and Churches, at: http://www.om.org/en/about/what-we-believe

The K.I.S.S. Principle

You will note that their website backs up the information provided in this email. The problem here is the inconsistency that could take place with the gospel message as it is presented from member to member. The email even states that there are disagreements within OM regarding this. This is confusing, because you would think that an organization such as this, that is trying to promote evangelism around the world would at least be consistent in its presentation of the salvation message they are trying to pass along. Apparently, by their own admission, the presentation of this most important message can vary from OM member to OM member depending on the denomination that member belongs to or is affiliated with.

While I don't believe that there should be any problem with trying to get people of various denominations and/or people groups to share the gospel message, so that many other people could be reached with this great message, I do believe that the message should be consistent and clear, so that they are confident that at the very least everyone is presenting the *same message of salvation* and that the message is based completely upon scripture. At times, this keeps us from linking up with various denominations and/or doctrinal views/positions, for the purpose of keeping the message clear and in tact.

PART IV

CONCEPT OF SCRIPTURE

Keep It Simple Servant

When considering the *Concept of Scripture* concerning salvation, it should be noted that while the Bible was penned down by around 40 different individuals, as they were inspired by God, ranging in status or social position from shepherd boys to kings, prophets, priests, fishermen, tax collectors, doctors, etc. over some 1600 years, containing information on creation, history, love, life, government, science and many other subjects, it has one main theme, "The Redemption of Man". This theme only has one answer to the question...*how can or must an individual be saved (or redeemed)* and that is by grace through faith in the finished work of Christ, alone on the cross for our sin.

The K.I.S.S. Principle

> For by grace are ye saved through faith; and that not of yourselves: *it is* the gift of God:
>
> Not of works, lest any man should boast.
>
> ~ Ephesians 2:8, 9

When Paul and Silas were in jail at Philippi, amid the tests they were enduring, they prayed and sang at midnight. Their rejoicing was not only wonderful from the standpoint that they realized the presence of the Lord amid their trial, but it was rewarded with an earthquake that loosened their bonds and opened the cell doors. The response of their jailor after assessing the condition of the jail and the situation he was in after the earthquake, with the potential for the prisoners to escape, leaving him to serve their sentences, was a simple, but direct and powerful question:

> …What must I do to be saved?
>
> ~ Acts 16:30

This is not only the most important question that could ever be asked, but the question that all people everywhere must ultimately have an answer to. Why, because how the individual responds to the answer to this question will determine where they will spend eternity. And, the Apostle Paul didn't mince words or provide a lengthy oratory or plan in answer to it. He simply stated:

Rev. Clayton Hampton

> ...Believe on the Lord Jesus Christ and thou shalt be saved...
>
> ~ Acts 16:31

What did the Philippian Jailor do? According to Acts 16:34, "*...he rejoiced, believing in God with all his house.*" He believed on the Lord Jesus Christ as Paul had advised him and was saved! The fact is, that God never intended for his great plan of salvation to be difficult to understand or experience. Man is the one that has complicated the message. Through the efforts of man to simplify this great message, he has instead made it more complicated, difficult to understand and require more effort to experience. God's message is simple, easy to understand and easy to experience. All that a person need do, as Paul stated is, "*...believe on the Lord Jesus Christ and thou shalt be saved!*" If you are wondering what to believe concerning the Lord Jesus Christ. Acts 16:34 acknowledges the fact that the Philippian Jailor believed that he was God. Then, the book of Acts is filled with Paul's account of what Christ did on the cross, which was pay for our sin. Therefore, believing that Jesus is God and that He paid for your sin appears to be what is being acknowledged here. Also, the word *believe* in Acts 16:31 is the Greek word πιστεύω (*pisteuō*), which means to have faith in or to trust in. Thus, the Philippian Jailor wasn't just acknowledging the fact that Christ paid for sin, but that he had placed his faith in Jesus as God and the one who had paid for *his* sins. He, in fact, was

The K.I.S.S. Principle

accepting Christ's payment for sin as his payment for his sins.

It should be noted at this point that while most every denomination or belief has a basic plan of salvation, where any number of statements and corresponding verses(in the Bible) will take an individual through a step by step or point by point list of information concerning salvation, explaining why a person needs to be saved, how and who provides it as well as how to attain or achieve it. But, what is not explained is that many times a person is already several steps into the process, mentally and/or spiritually, and should or could be approached at that point instead of starting with point/step 1. This could be what the Apostle Paul is referring to in I Corinthians 3:6, where he says, "...I have planted, Apollos watered; but God gave the increase." An individual, many times, will come in contact with several different individuals who will pass along the message of salvation to them and when we encounter them, they are already well aware of some of the information. And, this is what may have happened to the Philippian Jailor.

At this point, I would like to interject into the story of the Philippian Jailor, The Plan of Salvation that this author uses, when the person being witnessed to is unfamiliar with scripture(which is the case normally) and/or their state as a sinner(where many people believe that man is basically good) is:

Rev. Clayton Hampton

1. ALL men are sinners.
   – Romans 3:10, 23

2. The PAYMENT for SIN is DEATH.
   – Romans 6:23

3. Man must be PERFECT to
   enter Heaven.
   – Revelation 21:27

4. Man is not good enough to earn
   God's PERFECTION.
   – Ephesians 2:8, 9; Isaiah 64:6

5. Jesus made the payment for
   Man's SIN and gives man HIS
   righteousness.
   – II Corinthians 5:21

6. ALL that man MUST do to have
   ETERNAL LIFE is BELIEVE.
   – John 3:16, Romans 16:31

7. You can KNOW for sure,
   RIGHT NOW, that you have
   ETERNAL LIFE.
   – I John 5:13

Prayer:

Dear Lord Jesus, I admit that I am a
sinner and believe that you paid for my
sin. The best that I know how, I accept

The K.I.S.S. Principle

your payment for sin and am trusting
in your payment for sin as my payment
for my sin and I accept your free gift of
eternal life. Thank you! Amen!

Please note, that in the aforementioned plan,
there is no mention of a commitment to Christ, or
a turning of the person's life over to the Lord, etc.
That is because while the Lord does desire that we
serve Him, salvation is not based on those things,
but solely upon our faith in the finished work of
Christ on the cross as the payment for our sin.

That being said, according to this information, the
question that the Philippian Jailor asked, and the
Apostle Paul's response indicates that all the man
was in need of was point 6. He didn't need Paul
to tell him that he was a sinner. He knew it. He
didn't need Paul to tell him that his payment was
death. He knew that. He just wanted to know what
he needed to do to be SAVED. And, the Apostle
Paul obliged him in saying, "...*believe on the Lord
Jesus Christ and thou shalt be saved...*"

So, dear servant of the Lord, not only do I exhort
you to be cautious in how you present God's
greatest message, not cluttering it with the inter-
ests or ingenuity of man to make it more simple
or understandable than the Lord himself, but
keep in mind where the person you are talking/
witnessing to is in the process(if possible) and use
the *simple plan for salvation...*that the Lord laid
out in His Word.

Remember...

Keep **I**t **S**imple **S**ervant...

RECOMMENDED READING

First, and foremost, the Bible (A good translation, such as the King James Version, the New King James Version, the New International Version) is recommended.

It is recommended that you set aside a specific time of day, every day for reading your Bible. While you may want to read various different portions of scripture due to what you may be studying at the time, it is recommended that you read straight through from Genesis to and through Revelation each year.

Remember that while the books below have been recommended as additional reading resources, the only book that is inspired by God is His Word, the Bible! So, you may at times, find things in a recommended resource that you might question. Remember to use God's Word as the criteria for

The K.I.S.S. Principle

the judgment of material contained in a resource, not personal preference.

Handbook of Personal Evangelism, Stanford, Seymour, & Streib, Florida Bible College

All About Repentance, Seymour, Harvest House Publishers

Full Assurance, Ironside, Moody Press

Shall Never Perish, Strombeck, Moody Press

So Great Salvation, Strombeck, Moody Press

The Gift of God, Seymour, Grace Publishing Co

Bible Doctrines, Cambron, Zondervan

Rightly Dividing the Word of Truth, Scofield, Loizeaux Brothers

Printed in the USA
CPSIA information can be obtained
at www.ICGtesting.com
LVHW092038101023
760669LV00002B/18